MY NAME IS BUDDY

THE LIFE AND TIMES OF A FORMER CHILD STAR,
WHO NOBODY REMEMBERS.

Stephen Gustafson

JANE –
THANKS FOR
BEING A FAN –
STEVE G.

BookLocker

Saint Petersburg, Florida

A NOTE FROM THE AUTHOR

Let me begin by offering an apology. If you've picked up this book hoping to find your name mentioned or attached to one of my many adventures, and it's not here, I'm sorry. The hardest part of writing this memoir was deciding on what to tell and what not to tell. Even though there are many other layers to my story, it became clear that not every little detail was going to prove pertinent or necessary to the overall narrative. There were people I knew, friends, and girlfriends that came and went, and there were pets I had that meant the world to me. But not every single connection, relationship, or interaction merited inclusion.

I wanted this book to be about the core experiences and people that shaped my life and profoundly affected my soul. It's been a remarkable ride so far, but there was damage done. It didn't seem like it at the time because I got swept up in all the attention and adoration that came my way, but it sacrificed my childhood. It forced me to grow up before I should have, and it irrevocably tore my family apart. My parents are now gone, and as an only child, I've had no brothers or sisters to lean on when the stress and the pressures hammered down on me. I was supposed to be a 'good boy,' remember my lines, hit my marks, and be professional at all times. Bike rides, tossing a football, playing in the snow, fishing with my dad, and all the other things regular kids did in a normal upbringing were not mine to enjoy. I couldn't even attend traditional public schools in Connecticut because the kids (back then) didn't understand why I was treated differently. I was continually harassed, bullied, and even beaten up by kids who wanted money because I was 'supposedly' "Mr. Money bags" by being on TV. I was spat on, chased, and forced to embarrass myself in front of classes because the teachers didn't like the fact that at ten years old, I was making more money than they were. I lived in terror. For every standing ovation I received, for every award or accolade I was given, and for every special 'once in a lifetime experience' I had, a scar was left behind. My salary wasn't for jobs well done; it was combat pay for wounds inflicted by having been given too much, too soon. The hardest thing I had to accept was that it wouldn't last. Once the industry had gotten what it wanted from me, it left me high and dry, without the necessary skills to survive in the 'real world.' But survive I did, and this book tells the story of how I was able to overcome the odds and turn what at first was a positive and then a negative, back into a positive again.

I know it sounds like I'm bitter, but I'm not. It was as much my choice as it was my parents. I don't blame them, and I don't regret any of the sacrifices made in order to pursue a career that eventually flamed out after burning so brightly. When people ask me, "if you had the chance, would you do it all again?" Without hesitation, my answer is always unflinchingly the same, "Absolutely."

One final note on the chronology.

Most of what is presented here came from memory, with photographs, newspaper clippings, the internet, and materials my mother kept filling in the gaps. As with life, the unfolding events intersected and overlapped with each other. I've done my best to be as accurate as possible with dates, but not all of it is as precise as I would have liked. Sometimes you just have to go with the flow.

TABLE OF CONTENTS

OVERTURE

Over the years, many people have told me that I should write a book about my life because it hasn't exactly been normal. I've achieved fame, but I'm not famous. I have fans, but they wouldn't recognize me if they saw me on the street. People remember watching me on TV, but only after they find out what show I was on. Neither my name nor my face are instantly recognizable. I've been on Broadway, performed at Lincoln Center, Caesar's Palace, The Waldorf Astoria, and even on Royal Caribbean Cruise ships…. still, nobody knows me.

Like Forrest Gump, I've always seemed to be in places where history was being made by people and events around me that would shape the world. It's now the 25th of September 2020 and about 100 degrees outside here in Southern California. Fires are raging all over the State, ash is falling everywhere, and the sky looks like something right out of "MAD MAX." My wife and I have been self-quarantining since March with my parrot and our three dogs, so I couldn't think of a better time to sit down and write my memoir. I've just turned 62, and with fewer years ahead then there are behind, didn't want to miss the opportunity to finally document the adventure that has been my life. So, if you're interested in getting to know who I am and what I've accomplished, then by all means…. keep reading. I promise you it won't be dull.

ACT ONE: THE EARLY YEARS

On September 3rd, 1958, at 6:50 pm (EST) at New Britain General Hospital (CT), I came into this world to a set of parents who had absolutely no business being together. A case of opposites who fell prey to the standards of a 1950's 'Ozzie and Harriet' American lifestyle that insisted you get married, have children and live in a house with a white picket fence around it. Everything perfect as apple pie and ice cream.

My Mom circa 1956

My Mother, Joan Patricia Brodersen, was one of 4 daughters born to Kermit and Minnie Brodersen of Newington CT, and my father was one of four brothers born to Russel and Claire Gustafson of Manchester CT. Of the sisters, there was Joan (who was the oldest), then Ruth, Ellen, and Margaret. The brothers consisted of Russel Jr., Robert, Richard, and Ronald. Robert Earl Gustafson was my father. The Brodersen's were of Danish descent, and the Gustafson's were Swedish, so I guess that makes me a full-fledged Scandinavian Viking! My parents, Robert and Joan, met at a picnic during the summer of 1956, but I know little else as to what the occasion was or how they were introduced. What I do know is that eight months later, on January 5th, 1957, they were married, and 21 months after that, I came into being—a product of two vastly different temperaments, life interests, and values. Like I said, no business being together, let alone getting married and producing offspring.

My mother (Joan) was a well-educated young woman who read voraciously and was attending the Hart College of music. She had aspirations of being an Opera singer and spent a good deal of her time immersed in classical music, art, literature, and Theatre. My father (on the other hand) was a rabble-rouser who'd started smoking and drinking at the age of 15. He was immersed in sports, and despite his small stature (5ft.8"), he played semi-pro football and was known back then as a triple threat (Passing/Kicking/Running). He never pursued a Pro-career but instead ended up in Law enforcement as a beat cop in our hometown of Newington, CT. He'd served in the navy aboard an Experimental Destroyer (USS Harwood) during the Korean War and picked up bad habits that would define his life and relationships right up until his passing in 2010. My father was a good man with a kind heart, but alcohol brought out a mean streak in him that drove a wedge between him and my mother, and eventually me. I'll come back to this later, but for now, I'll keep the narrative moving forward on the timeline.

In keeping with my Scandinavian heritage, I was born with fine white hair, a fair complexion, and blue eyes. I must say that I was a lovely baby, the product of good genes from both sides. As I grew, I'd come to find out that I'd inherited my mother's passion for music, theatre, and the arts along with my father's 'street smarts.' It was an odd pairing, but then again, so were they. I'd garnered the best of both their worlds, and these traits would ultimately serve me well in the years to come.

My Mother was soft-spoken, patient, and attentive but struggled with the knowledge that having a child and a singing career was likely going to be an impossibility. She was a good Christian woman who abided by supporting her husband and maintaining a good home for her family. Having a professional career in Opera would no longer be an option. Dad was a 'solid guy,' respected by the community, committed to his job and responsibilities as both a husband and father. My parents were doing what they felt was right for the time, but I think, in hindsight, that my father's 'role' proved less suitable for him than my mother's did for her. She found contentment in raising me, and through her creative outlet as Director of the local Children's Theater program. My father found his in sports, beer, and cigarettes. He worked hard and played hard, but more often than not, without my mother's involvement.

My Grandfather Kermit (whose name was given to me as the 'K' in my initials SKG) was a master plumber, carpenter, and electrician. He, along with 2 of his brother's had built homes and an apartment complex that we lived in at the corner of Main St. and Hartford Ave. in Newington. For reference, Newington is a town in Hartford County, Connecticut, located about 8 miles south of downtown Hartford. Both my family and my mother's parents had apartments in the complex, so the convenient proximity of my Grandparent's made for close bonding and easy babysitting duties when needed. It was a great setup, and I have many fond memories of the times I spent with them.

Kermit was the spitting image of Santa Clause, and every year he would don his red suit and take his place at Santa's Workshop located in a barn at the

Eddy Farm. The farm was a historical treasure from the late 1800s and would get decked out in all of the season's finery, including a fabulous workshop complete with elves and toys. Children from all over the State would come just for a chance to sit on Santa's lap and tell him what they wanted for Christmas, with Kermit playing his role to the hilt. Some years later, when I was around 12 years old, Kermit would win a National contest for Santa Clause lookalikes! He got significant publicity, which only added to his seasonal popularity turning him into a legend and a local treasure adored by the entire town.

Until the age of three, what little memories I have can only be triggered by perusing old black & white photos kept in a box that's managed to move along with me over the years. It wasn't until age four when, after being hauled along to the Children's Theatre on a regular basis, did my mother decide to see if there was any latent talent lurking inside of me. On one particular day, she placed me in with a group of kids who were doing Theatre games (a method for training actors) and let me loose. I did something that everyone reacted to, and the next thing I knew, I had the part of the Littlest Grasshopper in a production of "Once Upon A Clothesline." It's a simple story about a giant black spider who lives in a tree and terrorizes two clothespins and their insect friends. Believe it or not, it was an award-winning play, and not nearly as dark and scary as my description makes it sound.

My father, bless his heart, ended up playing the part of the Spider (he was excellent), and I had my first taste of performing in front of an audience. The kicker to this was that during one of the rehearsals, I again did something that would ultimately become a scene-stealer. The bit ended up making me the most popular character in the show, with audience members dying to meet me afterward, and I was only four!

At that time, there was a Senator named Everett Dirksen, who was known for his deep gravelly voice. I'd heard him on the radio and TV and was able to imitate him. My only lines in the play were "Me too, Me Too!" which I spoke every time I lagged behind and wanted to catch up. For some reason, I used this voice during a rehearsal and sent everybody to the floor in hysterics! My mother was stunned and told me to leave it in. The rest was history. After that, she found a reason to include me in every production, which meant I got to travel around the Eastern Seaboard as the Newington Children's Theater had grown in popularity under my Mother's direction. My Grandfather had taken an old delivery truck and reworked it into a mobile stage with rotating sets that could be changed out to fit whatever show we were doing. It was a revolutionary idea, and each summer for the next three years, it allowed us to take our productions on the road and share them with other schools and Rec centers from Massachusetts to Maine. My Mother's work and dedication to the Children's Theatre also credited her performances in various community theater productions. She and I even performed together in "THE KING AND I," where she would use her singing skills as Mrs. Anna while I played one of the King's children!

Side note: *At the age of three, I appeared at the Bushnell in Hartford with Captain Kangaroo and the Hartford Symphony Orchestra. There were only two performances in which I played a Trenchcoated little Spy holding up the back end of a line of other taller Spies (very much like my role in 'Clothesline'). The audience, and the Captain, were so taken with me that during the 2nd performance, the Captain pulled me out of the line and held an impromptu one on one with me! Of course, the audience loved it, but I was so little that after I came off stage, I started crying because I thought they were all laughing at me. After the Captain and my mother explained that they were laughing 'with me' and not at me because my answers were funny, did I understand how I could affect an audience. It wasn't entirely clear to me as I was only 3, but over time, I would gradually come to understand and embrace the dynamic.*

Right around now, my father made Sergeant on the Police Force and was also the resident firearms instructor for both recruits and seasoned officers.

His duties kept him busy, but he always managed to find time to hang out with his buds at one of the local watering holes. This routine usually led to his coming home late and intoxicated, which resulted in yelling from him and tears from my mother over his behavior and his absence from dinner. It was a scene I would repeatedly see played out through the years and one that I'd one day become forced to intervene in when things eventually escalated to infidelity.

"ON BORROWED TIME"

As Director of the Children's Theater and a member of the Community Theater Players, my mother had contacts with other Directors and local Playhouses, some of which were very established and award-winning. One of those was the OVAL in Farmington CT. The OVAL was a summer Playhouse that did three productions each season and recruited talent locally and from Boston and New York. It was a small house that sat about 80 people and had the unique element of being a 'square.' The stage was in the center, and the audience sat around the set with the actors entering the space from the four corners. It was both intimate and challenging. Intimate for the audience because, at times, they could almost touch the actors and challenging for the performers who had to 'block-out' the patrons to avoid eye contact. Absolute focus was required to maintain the imaginary walls that were 'invisible' to the audience.

"ON BORROWED TIME" 1967

In May of 1967, my mother received a call from a Producer/Director friend of hers named Sam Capuano. Sam was looking for an eight-year-old boy that could handle a significant role in the production of Paul Osborne's 'ON BORROWED TIME" at the OVAL. He knew she had all ages of kids who were well trained and could probably handle a lead role. Well, she didn't. I was the only eight-year-old she had, and she wasn't sure I was up to something as challenging as a lead in a semi-professional production. What she did next was pretty clever. She told him she had a child but didn't tell him it was her son. If I was going to get the part, she didn't want any favoritism from him because I was her child. Mom scheduled the audition time, and several days later, I was in Sam's office in Hartford, reading some scenes from the play while mom waited outside.

After about ten minutes, he called my mother into his office. Not knowing what to make of how the audition went, mom sat down next to me and waited to hear the verdict. "I've got a feeling about this young man," he told her. "He's a natural and has good instincts. I'd like to use him for the show." There was a long pause before my mom finally spoke. "He's my son." She said. "I had a feeling that was the case," Sam responded, "But I didn't want to let on that I knew. He looks like you." My mother was beside herself. I still didn't understand the magnitude of what was happening or what would be expected of me, but it seemed like fun, so I went along with it because mom appeared to be so happy. For reference, The Play is about the relationship between a Grandfather and his Grandson (Pud) whose parents have been killed in a car crash, putting the Grandparents in charge of taking care of him. The Grandfather is keeping 'Death' a prisoner in his apple tree outside the home to prolong his life and have time to care for Pud. The ending is a real tearjerker, and not for the reason you think.

"ON BORROWED TIME" With Gramps, 1967

On Tuesday, July 18th, 1967, an 8-1/2-year-old named Stephen Gustafson took to the stage at the OVAL on the opening night of "ON BORROWED TIME." Two days later, the reviews would come out in the local papers.

"Mr. Murphy's (Gramps) moments with (Pud) Stephen Gustafson come off beautifully – easy, touching, shining. Half the credit for this goes to eight-year-old Master Gustafson, who is a natural on stage". FARMINGTON VALLEY HERALD

"Stephen Gustafson, as the Grandson, Pud, is equally remarkable, not only for the charm and ability of his tender years but for his complete naturalness." WETHERSFIELD POST

"Stephen Gustafson is a young actor who's on stage manner is assured without being aggressive, his mannerisms are natural without being assumed, and his delivery is accurate and sincere." THE HARTFORD TIMES

One reviewer even compared the chemistry between Gramps and me 'as reliable as Andy Griffith and Opie.' It was high praise indeed, and a nugget of trivia that I would, many years later, get to share with Andy in person!

The show was a resounding success that summer, even though, with only four performances remaining in the run, I came down with a case of the mumps! The Mumps can be very painful due to the swelling of the parotid salivary glands in the face just below the ears, and its contagion can be very dangerous for adults. It could cause sterility in adult males if they didn't have the virus as a child. So, with my illness a potential health risk, Sam called a cast meeting to determine if we should cancel the remaining performances. Sam first spoke with my mother since I was suffering and would likely be hindered by the discomfort. I didn't want to let anybody down and had a great time performing, so I told her I would continue if the rest of the cast wasn't concerned about catching it. The members of the troupe all looked at each other, and then 'Gramps' said, "Hell, if the kid can go on so can the rest of us, Mumps be damned!" and go on we did, without a hitch or anyone becoming infected.

Later, at the end of the summer season, the OVAL, along with the Farmington Valley Herald, held a ceremony to present select performers with accolades for their work. I was presented with the award for "Outstanding Performance and Best Newcomer of the Season. It was quite an honor for someone so young, and even now (53 years later), still means a great deal to me.

"MACBETH"

The next step in my career path came very quickly. It turned out that one of the cast members in 'On Borrowed Time" heard about a production in need of a young boy for a role at The American Shakespeare Theatre in Stratford CT. The Theatre was first formed in the early 1950s and was considered highly prestigious, with many big-name actors gracing its stage. In this instance, it was to be "MACBETH" under the direction of the Theatres former artistic director John Houseman. The man is a legend in the industry, so I won't attempt to provide his biography here. Just look him up on the web.

A phone call from Sam to the Theatre in Stratford clinched an audition, and off we went to see what would happen. The Theatre was about a forty-minute drive from our home in Newington and was visible from the Highway even though it sat back quite a bit on the property. It was a grand structure emulating its sister venue in London, England, and I can remember feeling awe-struck and intimidated by it as we drove up.

I was reading for the role of 'Young MacDuff' who, along with his Mother Lady MacDuff, is assassinated by McBeth's henchmen. I don't recall much about the actual audition except for the strangeness of the wording but somehow managed to impress them and was quickly cast in the role. Rehearsals began immediately, and we opened in mid-September. One unique aspect of this Theatre was the Q&A that was held with the audience after each performance. My participation was unplanned, but Mr. Houseman discovered very quickly that the audience was tremendously interested in making sure I was okay, due to the violent nature of the attack. It took only two performances before I was included in the Q&A to relieve the patrons that all was well with Young MacDuff.

*TRIVIA: The henchman who stabbed me twice daily during the performance was a New York actor named Richard Castellano. Five years later, Richard would play the role of 'Clemenza' in the "THE GODFATHER."

Unknown forces were clearly at work regarding the remarkable opportunities I'd been presented with, and things were about to take another leap as a full-blown professional career in New York now loomed on the horizon.

The actress who played Lady MacDuff suggested to my parents that the time might be right for me to get an Agent in NY since my career was starting to get some real traction. So, after discussing it between themselves, my folks sat me down to find out what I thought about it. I was having a great time with everything that was happening, but they wanted to be sure it was something that 'I' wanted rather than just doing it to please them. I said that as long as they were okay with it, so was I; besides, we all agreed we had to see just how far things would go. Based on all the feedback we were getting from other performers and the overwhelming audience response, we felt like we needed to see what might happen. For all we knew, it might turn out that this was all just a 'flash in the pan.' A legitimate NY Agency would undoubtedly prove to be the best judge of talent and future career opportunities if I really had something marketable.

A decision was made to reach out to the biggest, and best children's Agency NY had to offer to see if there was any interest in representing me. If we were going to do this, then we might as well shoot for the top. There was no sense in wasting time. If a professional career was to materialize, then this would be the best way to determine whether the path was worth pursuing or not. It would be a considerable commitment for my parents because it would require regular trips to Manhattan, which meant a driving time of over four hours round trip. A long way to go for what usually amounted to about 30 minutes of waiting and auditioning time.

NEW YORK

The Agency was called MARSHALL MANAGEMENT and was located on 58th St. just above Broadway. A high-rise on the west side, their offices were on the 14th floor and offered an excellent view of all the hustle and bustle that Spring of 1968 New York had to offer. Having never been that high up in a building before, I was fascinated by how much smaller everything looked from that height. Little did I know just how quickly that perspective would apply itself to my career once things began to really take off.

My parents and I sat in the waiting area adjacent to the receptionist for just a short bit before the lady at the front desk asked me to come into the large office behind her …. alone. If it were warranted, my parents would have the opportunity to meet with her after I was through.

The Agent's name was Loretta Marshall. She was a striking woman with white hair and a voice that immediately commanded your attention, crisp, clear, and all business. She indicated to me to take a seat, and I quickly saddled my tiny, 9-year-old body into the large leather chair in front of her desk. We spent the next 15 minutes just talking. She asked me about the shows I'd done and why I enjoyed performing so much and never once spoke 'down' to me like many adults would do when talking to a child. She never asked me to read anything, sing or recite something from memory like I would have at an audition. She just wanted to get to know me. After a bit, she buzzed the front desk and asked for my parents to come in and join us, which they promptly did.

After the introductions, she got right down to business. She told them that there had only been one other time in her history as an agent that she'd wanted to sign a child to a contract on the spot. This was going to be the second. My parents sat dumbfounded and were curious about why she felt so strongly about having me sign that day. She told them it was a gut feeling, and one she rarely felt with most kids that passed through her doors.

They might have talent but didn't have "it." She clarified that the "it" was something special and could only be determined by 'really' hearing what the child had to say. Singing, dancing, and reciting scenes were all very well, but you only got a sense of a child's real talent through a dialog that allowed for their 'true' personality to shine through. Personality was king. It's what the audience connected with. If you had that, then you had "it."

She suggested that the three of us step into her conference room so we could discuss the offer, but it seemed pretty clear that signing was a foregone conclusion. It was an outcome that none of us had expected. Still, it solidified all the feedback, advice, and positive encouragement that kept coming in from the Producers, Directors, and Actors I'd worked with over the past year. We had to see this through. We told Loretta that we'd sign and looked forward to my first opportunity to audition so we could prove her 'gut feeling' was right. It took less than 48 hours for that to happen.

The very next morning, Loretta's office called with an appointment scheduled for late in the day. I needed to be in NY at 4:00 pm to audition for a 9-week summer tour of "THE MUSIC MAN." I would need to sing a short song and read a scene from the script. I was so excited I positively burst into flames, and my folks were beside themselves that things were happening so quickly. Even if I didn't get the part, it still showed that having an agent proved to be a positive move. My Dad worked only half a day and then picked me up at 1:00 pm for our trip to NY and my first thoroughly professional audition.

The casting office was swarming with singers, dancers, actors, and all sorts of people who were auditioning for various summer touring shows. My previous casting calls had been tame compared to this, with only myself and the Director involved in the process. This experience was entirely something else! Once I checked in, they handed me the 'sides' I'd be reading and asked if I had my sheet music for the audition song. I gave the sheets to the young lady behind the desk, and she attached it to my picture and brief resume.

I went over and sat on a bench just outside the room where I'd be having my audition. My father hadn't come in with me as he was desperately trying to find a place to park the car, but because of all the talent in the office, finding space anywhere nearby was proving impossible.

After about ten minutes of waiting, they summoned me into the room where I met three people involved in the casting process, the Director, the Producer, and I think the Director's assistant. Everyone was cordial but business-like, and we jumped right in by reading the scene from the script. The assistant read the other person's lines, and when we finished, they asked me to sing the song I'd brought with me. There was a pianist in the corner who already had my sheet music, and he just started playing, which caught me off guard, but I jumped right in and gave it my best. Everyone thanked me and said they'd be in touch, and just like that, it was over. When I came out, my Dad was standing there looking disappointed because he'd wanted to be there with me before I went in. I told him I thought it went well, but it sure was different from the auditions I'd had with my first two shows. We spent the next two hours talking about it all the way home in the car.

My mother didn't quite know what to make of it, but she knew the big leagues were a different animal from local and regional theater casting calls. Very intense with a lot more competition. Show business in NY was about money and power, so you either stepped up and met the match or bowed out and quickly faded into obscurity.

She knew she should have warned me how it might be, but she'd always been one to let me experience things on my own. Allow me to handle myself and process and learn from the decisions I made, good or bad. So far, I'd been fortunate, but it had been in a protected environment with lots of people there to assist and support me along the way. If I sincerely wanted to be a performer on the big stage, I'd have to learn to take rejection and push through uncomfortable situations from time to time. Some people might think I was too young to have to make those kinds of choices, and that it was too much pressure to put on a child at this stage in his life. Maybe it was, but I chose it. My parents never pushed or insisted I do any of it. In fact, they'd gone out of their way to make sure I was enjoying myself, and if for any reason, I wanted to stop, I just had to give the word, and life would go back to whatever I wanted it to be. There was no pressure to keep going. It would last only as long as "I" wanted it to last.

While waiting for my dad and me to return home, mom answered another call from the Agency, indicating another audition the next day at the very same place for a production of "The Sound of Music." The call time was 11:00 am, so there would be a quick turnaround before heading back to NY 12 hours later. As you can see, the commute was already taking its toll, and I'd only gone Pro three days ago!

This time, for the return trip, my mother decided to tag along and see for herself what I'd described on our arrival back home the night before. Again, my father hunted to find a place to park while my mom accompanied me into the casting offices. We entered into the same amount of clamor and the same check-in routine as the day before. My mother took it all in stride as I led her to the bench I'd sat on the previous day, but before we could even sit down, I was motioned in for the audition. The same three people were there along with the pianist and one more. There was a beat, and the man I believed was the Director asked me what I was doing there again. He stood up, gave his assistant a look, then turned back to me. "Didn't anyone tell you got the part in "The Music Man" yesterday?" he asked. After a moment of stunned confusion, I said, "Not that I'd heard." He turned back to his assistant and told her, "Get this kid's Agent on the line. We need to straighten this out."

I stepped back outside the office and immediately relayed the news to my mother, who just smiled before ushering me outside to find my father. Dad was only a few paces down the street and walking towards us when she told him to get to a payphone and call Loretta because there'd been a lapse in communication between the casting office and the Agency. A moment later, the Assistant stepped up and told us we should head over to the Agency right away so Loretta could explain the mix-up. I was still trying to process what'd just happened, but Mom was in 'Director mode' and guiding everything along until we got to Loretta's where all was made clear. I had indeed landed the role of Winthrop, but the assistant had somehow missed making the call to her last night to let them know not to have me come in for "The Sound of Music" today. She said everyone at the casting office was apologetic and thanked us for forgiving the misunderstanding. She finished by leaning up against her doorway with a big smile and said, "I told you so, didn't I? I always trust my gut."

It was amazing. I'd landed my first Professional role right out of the gate. Rehearsals weren't scheduled to start for about eight weeks, but that didn't mean I'd be stagnant during that time. There would be only one week of rehearsal in June for music and blocking, which required me to learn my songs and dialog before we got there. This particular production was to star the stage and screen heart-throb John Raitt (Bonnie Raitt's Father) as Harold Hill. Ron Howard played the role of Winthrop in the 1962 Movie version, so once again, I seemed destined to have comparisons made just like there were from "ON BORROWED TIME." Winthrop played opposite a character named Amaryllis, who'd been cast with a young girl named Denise Nickerson. Denise and I would become good friends and would work together again in the not too distant future. Many may recall Denise's turn as Violet Beauregard in the 1971 film "WILLY WONKA & THE CHOCOLATE FACTORY," where she blew up into a blueberry chewing an experimental piece of bubblegum.

"THE MUSIC MAN" With John Raitt & Denise Nickerson, 1968

It was during this period, just before rehearsals started, that I also managed to book several TV commercials. Mattel, Pepperidge Farm, and Old London Cheese Doodles were among my first forays in front of the camera, and I loved every minute of it. Even Loretta was surprised by the fact that every audition I went on, I booked, which was unheard of for child actors at that time. I was quickly becoming the 'go-to' kid for just about everything, and my parents could hardly keep up with my demanding schedule.

By the last week in June, my mother and I had journeyed to Paintsville, MD, for the start of "THE MUSIC MAN" rehearsals while my father stayed in Newington to keep working and maintain the fort while we were away. This scenario would be the beginning of a string of such work/travel requirements that would distance my Mother and me from my father and have lasting effects on his relationship with both of us in the years to come.

Side note: "MAME," starring Angela Lansbury, was running on Broadway at the Winter Garden Theatre. A young man named Frankie Michaels (also represented by my Agency) was playing the role of Young Patrick Dennis (Mame's nephew, whom she is obliged to care for). After a lengthy run, Frankie had decided to leave the show and needed a replacement. My name came up and was seriously considered, but I was smaller than he was and deemed slightly too young for the role at that time. My Broadway debut would have to wait just a little bit longer.

"THE MUSIC MAN"

The Guber-Ford-Gross Co. circuit, as it was called back then, was a well-known tour of seven States that included Ohio, Washington D. C., Philadelphia, Massachusetts, and even the Oakdale Musical Theater in Wallingford, CT. The type of venues these tours performed in are no longer in use but stayed very popular during the '60s and '70s. Each locale was a huge tent that housed a graduating circular seating arrangement ending with a large round stage and an orchestra pit at the bottom. It was known as 'Theater in the round,' allowing the audience to have an unobstructed view of the performance no matter where they sat. A series of aisles that ran from the ground-level entrance of the tent to the bottom at stage level provided the patrons with access to their seats, and the performer's a means to step onto the stage. The aisles created wedge-shaped 'sections' for the audience to sit all around the production, which meant that sets were minimal and blocking and choreography had to present itself to all sides of the space. Entrance timing for the actors was essential based on the distance from the top of the aisle to the stage and was timed to prevent performers from lingering too long on the stairs next to the audience. It was also dangerous. One wrong move, and you could easily find yourself going headfirst down a long flight of cement steps. Certainly not acceptable by today's standards, but this was the 60's and safety for cast members wasn't always a primary concern back then.

"THE MUSIC MAN" With Denise Nickerson, 1968

Denise Nickerson was about 18 months older than I was, but we quickly bonded since we were the only two kids in the show. With this being my first big-time musical, I was captivated by the intricate music and dance routines. During our off-stage time, Denise and I would learn the choreography for the numbers and stand outside the tent, emulating the dancers in perfect unison. It was a blast and, to this day, remains an especially fond memory.

Another extraordinary moment happened about two weeks into the run when right in the middle of the song "The Wells Fargo Wagon," Mr. Raitt stopped the show by waving off the conductor of the orchestra. During this number, I'm supposed to run down into the middle of the crowd and start singing. The microphones that hung down over the stage from way up high weren't picking me up because I was so small and was hemmed in by the other players. John chose this exact moment to correct the problem. He walked over, picked me up, and placed me on the shoulder of the tallest dancer we had. The man was about 6ft 5inches tall, and with me now sitting on his shoulder, my face was directly in front of the mike! John walked back over to the conductor and told him to play and then turned to me and said, "SING!" The audience went nuts. The applause must have lasted for half a minute, and from that point on, I would run onto the stage, leap into the dancer's arms, and get hoisted on his shoulder so I could sing my part and the audience could hear me!

"THE MUSIC MAN" Microphone moment, 1967

John Raitt was larger than life. Men admired him, and women adored him. Every night after the show, John would take to the stage and sing 3 or 4 of his signature songs for the audience as an encore. When he hit High-C at the end of the last one, the house would go wild with applause that seemed to last for days. John, along with Howard Keel, were two of the largest male voices of the time, and their fans were plentiful. Indeed, John had an ego, but he was well-liked and always had the cast's (and the show's) best interests at heart. After we closed, he invited my parents and me to his home in the Hamptons. We had a barbecue, and I met his daughter Bonnie, who would later establish a remarkable Grammy-winning career of her own as a singer/songwriter and activist.

With the Oakdale Music Theatre on our list of stops, my father and both sets of Grandparents were finally able to attend and see me in a big show. Initially, my mother's parents weren't keen on my being in show business. They were Protestant Christians who were convinced that show business was a bad influence and would do me more harm than good. But, after seeing me in a few productions and how much I loved it, they began to soften. My Grandpa Brodersen ultimately became one of my biggest supporters, always making sure to come to see me whenever I was performing in New York or other local venues.

"OUR TOWN"

"THE MUSIC MAN" completed its run at the end of August that year, and two days after our return, I auditioned for and secured the role of 'Wally Webb' in a revival production of "OUR TOWN." Martha Scott, who'd played the role of 'Emily' in the original 1938 Broadway production and subsequent film version in 1940, had gathered a star-studded cast to bring it to life. The likes of Henry Fonda, Estelle Parsons, John Beal, Jo Van Fleet, John McGiver, Robert Ryan, and Kitty Wynn rounded out the cast.

Scott, Fonda, and Ryan had recently formed a standing repertory company called the Plumstead Players to kick off this 30th-anniversary production of the play and then continue with other shows utilizing this immense talent pool. I was truly fortunate to be a part of something so prestigious and would ultimately form some very special relationships with Broadway and Hollywood's biggest names.

"OUR TOWN" was scheduled to open on September 24th, 1968, at the new Plumstead Playhouse in Mineola, NY, and the Playwright 'Thornton Wilder' was going to be attendance! Because of the remarkable cast, every performance for the entire run had sold out even before we'd opened. My parents were both in disbelief. Here I was, this now 10-year-old kid performing alongside Hollywood legends that they'd grown up watching on stage and screen! My father was particularly taken with Robert Ryan as he was the quintessential 'man's man,' and my father respected his image and stature as a name in the business. What most people didn't know was that Robert had always wanted to be a dancer rather than an actor. He secretly practiced routines in his off time and had exceptional tap dancing and soft shoe skills. I'd been taking dance lessons since I first signed with Marshall Management, and every night after the show came down, Robert and I would sneak out onto the stage and do routines together. With only the single-stage manager's light illuminating us while we danced together, my father, who came to see many performances of the play, would stand at the back of the

Theatre in the dark and watch the two of us. It was like a dream for him. There was his son dancing with a screen legend like it was the most natural thing in the world. They became moments that he would always bring up in conversation with his friends because they were so special to him. He was so proud of my accomplishments but longed for the kind of intimate time with me that created a strong bond between a father and his son. The image of him standing alone, watching in silence at the back of the playhouse would become a metaphor for the remainder of our time together.

With "OUR TOWN" now under my belt, it was now time for my first go at playing Young Patrick Dennis in "MAME."

"MAME"

Early in 1969, I'd stayed busy doing more TV commercials and going on more auditions. One such casting call was for another 10-week, multiple city run of the Hit Musical "MAME." John Bowab was the Director, and he cast me in what would be the first in a series of "MAME" productions over the next several years. This one was to star Janis Paige in the lead role. Janis was one of the last surviving stars of Hollywood's Golden age with real stardom coming for her in 1954 as the character 'Babe' in the Broadway production of "The Pajama Game."

TRIVIA: Janis starred opposite John Raitt in 'The Pajama Game,' and the show was choreographed by none other than Bob Fosse.

"MAME" With Janis Paige, 1969

Rehearsals started in June, and the production would be presented in the same 'Theater-in-the-round' format used for "THE MUSIC MAN." We opened in Mid-July and ran right to the end of September. "Mame" was an ambitious show with a large chorus and elaborate dance numbers that had to be revised for a round stage rather than the usual proscenium. John Bowab was great to work with, and Janis a delight. I remember she could be moody, but she was always professional and treated me like her own child, which only added to our chemistry on stage. It was also the first time I'd work with a very funny and talented singer named Hazel Steck. Hazel was from Texas and had a singing voice that rivaled that of Kate Smith's, and like Smith, was something of a 'large' woman with ample bosom that entered the room before she did. I would later work with Hazel again in another production of "Mame," but she wound up marrying my Grandfather's brother Alwyn and ultimately became my Aunt and a member of my family!

During this road trip run, my mother received a phone call from Loretta, who told her she'd just gotten off the phone with Martha Scott. Due to the unprecedented response in Mineola, Martha had received a green light to take "OUR TOWN" to Broadway. The show would start with a two-week run at the Coconut Grove in Miami, FL, and then open in NY on November 25th at the ANTA Theatre for a five-week limited run. Martha wanted to have the original cast return for the production, but some of the original players had made other commitments and couldn't participate. Fonda would return as the 'Stage Manager,' but new famous faces would fill out the additional open roles. We would now be joined by Ed Begley (Sr.), John Randolph, Mildred Natwick, Irene Tedrow, John Fiedler, Margaret Hamilton, and Elizabeth Hartman. Margaret was best known for her role as the 'Wicked Witch of the West' in "THE WIZARD OF OZ," and Elizabeth was an Academy Award and Golden Globe Best Actress nominee for her role opposite Sidney Poitier in "A PATCH OF BLUE.' I would once again be playing Wally Webb (Elizabeth's Brother), but Elizabeth had prominent Red hair, so I was burdened with having to dye mine to match hers for the run of the show.

"MAME" came to an uneventful close at the end of August, and like with John Raitt, Janis invited us to her home in Upstate NY for a couple of days of R&R before heading back home and then onto Miami and Broadway!

"OUR TOWN" Pt. 2

The Coconut Grove Playhouse had initially been constructed as a movie theater called the Player's State Theater, and opened on January 3, 1927, as part of the Paramount chain. The movie house was conceived by the architect Richard Kiehnel of Kiehnel and Elliott. In the 1950s, George Engle, an oilman, bought it and spent over $1 million in renovations having the architect Alfred Browning Parker convert it to a live theatre. We rehearsed there for two weeks before opening, which was tat amount to two weeks of dress rehearsals before moving to Broadway.

The new cast members were terrific, and I became especially fond of Margaret Hamilton. She was absolutely nothing like her character from 'OZ.' We had this little routine where I would suddenly appear in the doorway of her dressing room, holding a large glass of water. She would jump to her feet and start screaming, "I'm melting! I'm melting!" then grab a janitor's broom and chase me out! Everyone loved it, and it became a running joke throughout the run.

By this time in my career, it had become necessary for us to rent an apartment in Manhattan. I was spending most of my non-touring time there, and having a place in the city made things easier for my father. My mother, as always, stayed with me through everything while my father would do his best to take time off from work and visit us wherever the show happened to be at that time. As a professional actor, I'd been earning a sizable salary, which my Parent's made sure was being put away for my future, but there were expenses, and some of my earnings were needed to cover them. Money for the singing lessons, dancing lessons, clothes, and the apartment had to come from somewhere. The hard thing for my father to swallow was that I was making a lot more than he was at eleven-years-old, and most of his colleagues knew it. I wasn't aware of this at the time because he never discussed it, and I had no reason to ask. So, it never occurred to me that the costs for him to fly out to wherever I was, and visit wouldn't have been possible without my salary. His pride and self-esteem were taking a beating, and I was utterly unaware of it.

Once we got back to NYC from Miami, we had a couple of days to settle in and prepare for the opening, but as usual, Loretta had set up some meetings for me to attend. The most important one was with Producers Fryer, Carr, and Harris via the William Morris Agency. Loretta had pitched them on using me for their upcoming production of "MAME" at Caesar's Palace in Las Vegas! It was a new idea to introduce a Broadway-level show into the main room of the Casino as most shows there were of the 'variety' type or individual big marquee names like Dean Martin or Frank Sinatra. The format was always two shows a night (an early one and a late one) with about a 3-hour break between the two. These producers were certain that with a little cutting and trimming of songs and dialog, a roughly 90-minute version could fill these slots and offer the gambling patrons something different from the same old 'Rat Pack' presentations. "MAME" was to be the first of this new concept.

As it turned out, the role of Patrick Dennis had already been filled by Shawn McGill, who was most likely the son of somebody close to one of the producers. They did, however, need someone to play the role of Peter Dennis (Older Patrick's son), who appears at the end of the show. The caveat to this was that I would also be the understudy for Young Patrick and given 'guaranteed performances' in the role throughout the six-month Casino commitment. To be fair, Shawn had done the part before and was a more than capable performer.

I had never been an understudy before, but the opportunity and prestige of playing opposite Hollywood legend Susan Hayward (as Mame) was something Loretta thought was worthwhile and would offer terrific PR going forward. The Producer's agreed, and I was cast that day without an audition. The reviews I'd received from my previous run with Janis Paige were apparently enough to satisfy their decision. I could hardly believe that I was about to open on Broadway and then make my debut in 'Sin City' Las Vegas. It was unreal. I was 11-years old!

"OUR TOWN" opened as planned, and, like the previous run-in Mineola, tickets had immediately sold out for the entire 5-week engagement. Audiences were anxious to see such an incredible collaboration of actors perform a play considered an 'American classic.' John Randolph and Irene Tedrow played my parents (the Gibbs). Irene was a twice nominated Emmy award actress, and John was a familiar face to the stage, screen, and television, and in 1987 would win the Tony Award for his performance in Neil Simon's "BROADWAY BOUND."

"OUR TOWN" With John Randolph & Irene Tedrow, 1969

John and I bonded rather quickly as I listened to stories about his life and the fact that both he and his wife had been blacklisted during the McCarthy era, nearly destroying their careers. John became my surrogate 'father' and took me under his wing. I learned a lot from him, and our relationship lasted for many years after the show closed.

One surprising friendship that sprang up during the run was the friendship my father made with Ed Begley. Ed was originally from Hartford, and the common ground the two of them shared kept them engaged with each other whenever there was a free moment.

Side Note: On April 27^{th,} 1970, Ed Begley wrote a brief letter to my parents and mailed it. On April 28^{th,} he unexpectedly passed away from a heart attack. The letter would be the last thing he wrote before he died. For years I'd held onto that letter hoping against hope that one day I would cross paths with his son Ed Begley Jr. and be able to share it with him. Last year in 2019, while having my car serviced in Van Nuys, I saw him sitting in the Chevy dealers showroom. I couldn't believe my luck and approached him. I introduced myself and then carefully broached the subject of his Father's passing and the letter I had in my possession. He asked if I could scan and send it to him. After digging it out from my storage unit, I did just that. It took 49 years, but I was finally able to keep my promise!

What can one say about HENRY FONDA? The man was a screen legend and everything you could hope him to be. It was now the 2nd time I'd worked with him, and our relationship just picked up right where we left off in Mineola. He was called 'Hank' by his close friends, but I always addressed him as 'Mr. Fonda' since I was a kid, and it would have been inappropriate for me to refer to him otherwise. He always smiled when I said 'Mr. Fonda' and always seemed interested in engaging with me whenever we had the chance to talk. It was during this run that his adult children, Peter and Jane, would come to see the show, and Henry made sure I came to his dressing room so I could meet them. They were wonderfully pleasant and full of praise for my performance, with Peter telling me that he'd also played my part when he was my age.

Because we'd opened right at Thanksgiving time, Henry wanted to make sure that the cast and crew enjoyed the holiday meal. So, he made arrangements with 'Sardi's' Restaurant to close it just for us to gather and share Thanksgiving as a theatre family. 'Sardi's' was a famous continental dining establishment located in the heart of the Broadway Theatre district and attracted all the biggest names in the industry. For Henry to have them close it for a private party was a big deal, not to mention having them change their regular menu to accommodate the needed Thanksgiving trappings for us. It was a great gathering, and later in the evening, Henry presented me with a personalized gift from Tiffany's – a sterling silver pocketknife with "OUR TOWN" and my name engraved in it. I still have it and polish it regularly, to keep its sheen and my fond remembrance of receiving it from him alive.

During the run, there was one moment of panic that occurred that only my mother and the Stage Manager were aware of. The 3rd act of the play ran about 40 mins and took place in a cemetery. The time is nine years after George and Emily have married. The characters who have passed on during this time are seated in chairs positioned on stair-like risers. The risers allowed the audience to see who had died along with Emily, who'd passed away during the birth of her second child. Those of us known as 'the dead' must sit absolutely still for the entire act until the lights go out, and the curtain closes.

"OUR TOWN" Cemetery Scene, 1969

One night, with my mother attending in the audience, I fell asleep on stage! The combination of being overtired and the low glare of the stage lights finally took their toll on me. So, after about fifteen minutes of fighting to stay awake, I succumbed to slumber. My head dipped into my chest as I fell asleep, and my mother was the only one in the audience who knew what'd happened. She quickly vacated her seat and rushed backstage to see the stage manager standing in the wings just off to my right, desperately trying to 'loud whisper' me back to consciousness! For the next 18 minutes, the two of them tried everything they could to wake me that wouldn't alert the audience, or the performers on stage, that I was out cold. The act was ending, the lights were going down, and as if on cue, I immediately woke up to see the curtain lowering. With perfect timing, I stood up and exited the stage with all the others as if nothing had happened. To this day, no one except my mother and the stage manager ever knew of the incident. Naturally, neither of them ever said a word to anybody for fear of freaking out the cast or causing them concern that it might happen again. Which, of course, it didn't.

With the Vegas production of "MAME" opening on December 27th, I was now having to attend rehearsals for it during the day and perform in "OUR TOWN" at night. It made for long days and late nights, but I was relishing every minute of it. My Mother coordinated all the scheduling details and was beginning to impress Loretta with her knowledge and patience in the handling of all of it. To keep things moving, I did my part, went where I was told, wore what I was told, and behaved as I should- always professional with my peers. I'd become the perfect 'little man.' But my childhood was anything but typical and was rapidly getting cut short because of the path my life was taking. I believe that if I'd not been an only child and had a sibling close to my age, none of this would have happened. Having a Brother or a Sister would have made it impossible for my mother to be in two places at once and favor one of us over the other. It would have been unfair to the entire family. As it stood, it was my father who was getting the short end of the stick, and in hindsight, I can now better understand how abandoned and uninvolved he must have felt. Always watching from the sidelines and never having the time with me to play catch, go fishing, take in a ballgame, or just hang out together.

I know there was so much he wanted to share with me, show me, and experience with me. Instead, I was the one sharing, showing, and experiencing while he became just one small part of my grander world. My Mother and I were bonding in a way he and I never would. She'd become my best friend and had found that my career was now her career, providing her with a surrogate for the Operatic one she'd one day hoped to have. It wasn't unhealthy, just a natural by-product of events that were unfolding. We were a great team, and fantastic things beyond her wildest dreams were happening. It was easy to get swept up in all 'elbow-rubbing' and attention given to her son by such famous people, even if it was at the expense of her marriage.

"MAME" Pt.2

The time between the closing date of "OUR TOWN" and the opening date of "MAME" posed a problem for the "OUR TOWN" production. Loretta would have to find a replacement that could cover my last 8 performances because I needed to be at Caesars Palace a week before opening to work with the complicated set pieces. Martha Scott wasn't happy but understood the situation, and a replacement was found just in time for my departure.

A TWA 747 had been chartered by the producers to fly the entire cast from NY to Las Vegas, and what a flight it was! The main cast had received 1st class seats with the chorus and secondary cast members relegated to coach, but that set-up didn't last long. No sooner were we in the air, seat belt signs off, did Susan pull back the curtains that separated the two compartments and announced that we were all just one big happy family, and everyone should feel free to mingle without class distinction! She was a firecracker, a tiny package of talent and goodwill infectious to everyone around her. A cheer went up in coach, and then minutes later, drinks were flowing via the stewardesses, and a steady stream of tobacco smoke floated above the top of the cabin like a thick mist of cotton candy. After all, it was 1969, and smoking was still very much the cultural norm. It would take more than thirty years before NO SMOKING laws would come into being, and another ten years after that, when indulging in this habit would become anathema to pretty much everyone.

As the drinks kept coming, the members of the chorus began to loosen up, with the singing of show tunes and impromptu attempts at dancing in the plane's aisles popping up. The first three hours of flight time were total showbiz mayhem until the alcohol and frivolity caught up, and the players fell into the quiet bliss of sleep. Cabin lights had been lowered, and those who were still awake were conversing and reminiscing about past shows they'd done. I could hear lines being quoted, snippets of songs being sung at low volume, and laughter from joke-telling and casual flirtations. These were theater people. These were my friends, my playmates, my teachers. They influenced my life and left indelible marks on my psyche that would stay with me forever. Even then, I knew I was part of something special and that I was right where I belonged.

Vegas of 1969 was a very different place than today's modern Vegas. It was still a playground for adults and adults only. Not the family-friendly 'Disneyland' that it portrays now. The gambling, the strip shows, the club acts, and pretty much everything else was geared for adults, with 'kids' not even factoring into the equation. Families didn't come here; only grownups came here to indulge in all the vices that grownups found enjoyable. Vegas in 1969 was still very much the Vegas that Bugsy Siegel had started in the late 1940s, only more so.

The 'strip' was a lot less 'dense' then it is today. Hotels were spread out with loads of Desert space in between. Only 'Downtown' offered close quarters with the lesser bars and casino's sharing blocks of brick and mortar. There was a movie theater down there and an actual 'Mall' (one of the 1st) near the Airport. There were horseback rides and an Ice rink for skating, but that was pretty much it when it came to stuff that would appeal to kids. One issue that required an immediate solution was that children were not allowed in the Casino or anywhere near the slots or gambling tables. Kids could walk around the periphery, but that was it. Here is where management at Caesars came up with a brilliant idea. Since both Shawn and I were performers in the Hotel, we were, in essence, employees, and as employees, had to have access to all areas of the complex. So, we were provided with Caesars Palace nameplates that we could wear that would allow us to roam anywhere on the premises without restriction! At first, it took some of the Hotel staff off guard, but eventually, they warmed to us. Sometimes they'd even go out of their way to engage us about the show and what it was like working in Las Vegas at such a young age. To put it another way, we became very cool cats at the Palace.

Susan Hayward was the only cast member who had a residence in the Hotel. The rest of the cast and crew were furnished with long term housing adjacent to the Casino. When I say adjacent, I mean a small apartment complex that sat across an expanse of desert to the left of the Palace about 75 yards across. The dome and shopping plaza that are there now didn't exist. Instead, there was an open parking lot and a pool/cabana set-up. Pretty mundane by today's standards, but impressive to all of us at that time. When we had to be at the Hotel, we would just walk across the desert, through the parking lot, and enter via an employee entrance near the rear. It was an easy and convenient arrangement. The only thing we had to be careful of was snakes.

No expense was spared to make the show a grand event. The set's, the costumes, the 30-piece Orchestra, and Susan Hayward were all there to dazzle an audience and hopefully get them to gamble even more money in the Casino. You spend a lot to make a lot was the mantra of every Hotel/Casino on the strip, and it was clearly visible by the names gracing the giant marquees that stood like monoliths in front of each of them. Juliet Prowse at the Flamingo, Howard Keel and Kathryn Grayson at the Dune's, Wayne Newton at the Aladdin, the list went on and on. Speaking of Howard Keel and Kathryn Grayson, when I was touring with the "MUSIC MAN," they were also on the same circuit, with their production of "THE FANTASTIKS" coming in on the heels of our show. I'd had the pleasure of meeting them on more than one occasion, so when I was in Vegas, they invited me to see their show. I had a front-row seat, and Howard broke from his performance to introduce me to the audience as an up and coming performer who could be seen nightly at Caesars Palace. I'd become a famous Vegas performer without even knowing it!

I'll bet you're wondering about my schooling at this point. Was I getting an education? The answer is yes. During the summer, it was never an issue, but the rest of the year, it was mandatory that I engage in some sort of regular curriculum. Since living and working in Manhattan had become a full-time thing, Loretta suggested that I enroll at Lincoln Square Academy. LSA had exclusively been designed to offer classes for kids who were working in show business. The hours were such that your day was short enough to accommodate auditions and rehearsals and still provide the needed subjects for school board requirements. You could even work via correspondence if you weren't performing locally or were on location for an extended period. The latter was how it worked for me while I was in Vegas. The production provided a tutor that spent three hours a day taking Shawn and me through the lessons provided by our schools. During breaks, we would play touch football in a section of desert just across the strip from the DUNE's Hotel.

Before MAME, Susan Hayward had very minimal singing experience. For the film "I'll CRY TOMORROW," she did her own singing but disliked the sound of her voice so much that Jane Froman dubbed her in the 1952 film "WITH A SONG IN MY HEART." Even without singing, her performance won her the Golden Globe that year for Best Actress in a Comedy film. Later, in 1958 she would win the Best Actress Oscar for her portrayal of Barbara Graham in "I WANT TO LIVE."

"MAME" With Susan Hayward, Las Vegas 1970

On-screen, Susan always looked tall, or taller than she was in real life, but she was all of 5 feet 3 inches in height. Traditionally, 'Mame Dennis' had mostly been played by women of taller stature (5' 8") and above. It was by no means a detriment to her taking on the role, as she was such a firecracker and a powerhouse of personality that no one cared about the height deficit. Another interesting fact about this production was that the actress cast in the role of 'Agnes Gooch,' Patrick's nanny was, a then-unknown, Loretta Swit! But more on that later.

The typical running time for "MAME" had always been around 2 hours and fifteen minutes, including a ten-minute intermission. Pairing this down to 90 minutes to fit the Casino's allotted time restriction was no mean feat. Certain scenes and several songs had to be either altered or deleted without hampering the telling of the story. In my opinion, the changes made in no way diminished the quality of the show, and actually improved the pacing and urgency of the unfolding events.

With a three-hour break between the early show and the late show, Shawn and I would often go off and explore our surroundings. One such exploration would lead to our discovery of a small entertainment venue known as "Nero's Nook," located near a bar on one side of the central casino area. 'The Nook' turned out to be presenting a topless ice show, and despite our 'employee status' was most definitely off-limits to a couple of inquisitive 11-year-olds. Of course, where there's a will, there's a way, and it turned out that one of the spotlight operators on our show also operated the spot for the Nooks ice show. He'd heard about our little discovery and invited us to come up into the booth, where we wouldn't be seen by management, and watch the show. He didn't have to twist our arms. The very next show he worked, we found ourselves sitting in the booth with a bird's eye view of (as I called it) the 'Booby Show.' Both of us felt like we had died and gone to booby heaven.

By today's ultra-PC standards, it would've been scandalous for us to have been caught viewing a show like this in a major Casino like Caesars. But this was Vegas of 1969, and as I said earlier, oversite and moral standards were almost non-existent. If no one complained or made a fuss about it, then to management, it never happened and was quickly forgotten about. My mother knew I'd seen the show but was always open about my sexual curiosity. She didn't want me growing up thinking that sex or sexual imagery was taboo or considered "bad," and something you should avoid because Satan would take your soul. Besides, I was in show business, and being exposed to semi-naked or half-undressed people was pretty much the norm due to dressing room space and off-stage costume changes. Explanation of the birds and the bees with my father had come early to prepare me for what my career experiences might reveal. Copies of 'Playboy' were not off-limits, so I formed a healthy appreciation for the female form at a slightly younger age than most young boys did. It was this 'appreciation' that made me go back to the 'Booby Show' about a dozen more times before losing interest.

"MAME" With Susan Hayward, Las Vegas, 1970

As the 'Star' of the show, Susan's dressing room was situated just off stage right. Many times, during the break, I would come down from my DR on the floor above, and we would play Gin Rummy together. She was still mourning the loss of her 2nd husband, Floyd Eaton Chalkley, which was evident even during rehearsals in New York. I think she enjoyed spending time with me as it proved to be both a distraction from his passing and fulfilled some of her nurturing needs as a mother because one of her sons was serving in Viet Nam. On one particular evening, I came down to play cards, but when I knocked on the door, she yelled out that she was on the phone trying to reach her son in Nam. Back then, this could prove to be a lengthy process as there were no cell towers or cell phones, and everything would have to be routed via landlines. With him being out in the DMZ, it could take hours to make a connection, and she wanted to stay focused on the task. Susan poked her head out and asked me to entertain her guest who'd come to see the show that night. I said, "Okay," and turned to see who I'd be 'entertaining.' My eyes first caught a glimpse of his patent leather shoes, and as I continued to scan upwards past the tuxedo pants and the tuxedo jacket, I found myself staring into the face of Charlton Heston. OMG, I thought to myself...." It's Taylor from PLANET OF THE APES"!

"Chuck," as he preferred to be called, extended his hand for a shake and said, "It's a pleasure to meet you, I enjoyed your performance and think I may have some competition coming up behind me." I was speechless. As an 11-year-old, my knowledge of him as an actor was pretty limited. I knew he'd played Moses and Judah Ben-Hur, but I was more interested in his work from POTA! He next suggested that we grab a bite to eat since Susan would be a while, so we headed off into the Casino where there was a sort of 'diner/coffee shop near the hotel entrance. He indicated to the star-struck hostess that we needed a table, and we were carefully escorted to a small booth near the back of the eatery, for privacy. I hardly remember the next 2 hours. I must have bombarded him with a thousand questions about "APES" and managed to squeeze a few in about "BEN-HUR" and "THE TEN

COMMANDMENTS," but I hadn't seen either of them all the way through, so I didn't want to seem like a fool who hadn't done his homework.

We'd finished eating long before we finally left the restaurant and headed back to find that Susan had completed her call and was wondering just where the heck we'd been all this time. Chuck apologized, and she invited him into her dressing room. She gave me a big smile and said, "Thanks," while Chuck thanked me for "An entertaining conversation." They disappeared inside, and I floated back to my DR upstairs. Later, after I'd told my mother what'd happened, she nearly passed out trying to imagine how an 11-year-old could have possibly kept someone of Heston's fame and stature, interested in a conversation for almost two hours! He most certainly must be a very patient man.

As was promised by the shows Producer's, I was allowed to perform in the role of Patrick Dennis at least once a week. It was during one of these performances that my 2nd on-stage panic moment occurred. At the beginning of the 2nd act, Young Patrick is now at boarding school and is seated in front of a typewriter working on a letter to Mame. The set was designed to rotate at a specific point in the song, indicating the passage of time and revealing a grown-up version of Patrick typing and singing the remaining lyrics of the melody I'd started. For some reason, a couple of stagehands thought it would be funny to type swear words and other assorted nonsense on the paper pre-inserted into the typewriter. As the lights came up, I glanced at the page and was so shocked by what I saw that I went blank and couldn't remember the lyrics. The Orchestra Conductor kept playing even though I wasn't singing, and eventually, the only thing I could think of doing was to hum. I hummed until the set rotated, and older Patrick picked up with the rest of the song, but I was devastated. I stepped off the turnstile with tears flowing down my face. I was always obsessed with knowing all my lines and, until now, had never 'gone up' while on stage. Chorus members rallied around me backstage to offer support, but I was inconsolable. In my mind, I'd screwed up and let everyone down. I was probably never going to be allowed to play the part again, and my mother would be furious with me.

This incident would prove to be a defining moment for me. I had to come to terms with the fact that I wasn't perfect, and that 'concentration' was paramount at all times on stage and to never allow distraction to affect your performance. Yes, I was overly hard on myself, but the sheer fact that I was even aware of this dynamic was proof that I was growing up fast and learning far more from my 'real world' experiences then I could ever hope to learn in a classroom. The 'kid' might be how the world perceived me, but the person inside was quickly outgrowing the child-like exterior. It was a self-perception complex that would haunt me well into my 20's and never fully resolve itself until I was much older.

Of course, the two stagehands responsible for the prank were severely reprimanded, and I still went on as Patrick moving forward. "Going-up" was a common occurrence that even the most experienced actor would experience from time to time. The rule of thumb was 'just forget about it and move on.' My mother knew it would happen at some point but was more concerned about my emotional well-being then she was about anybody being upset because I 'blanked' over a deliberate act of stage sabotage.

My father managed to find the time on several occasions to come west for extended visits, which was great but ultimately a bit strained. The weeks and months apart from us were taking its toll, and Vegas wasn't exactly the best place for someone with a drinking problem to hang out. My parents did their best to put on a 'good showing' that everything was OK between them, but the simmering resentment and jealousies from my father were starting to boil over. So, instead of pretending that we were one big happy family, he would head back home before things got ugly.

We spent Christmas and New Year in Vegas, which was quite the experience. Another decade had dawned with 1969 becoming 1970 and the beginning of another whole new chapter in my burgeoning career. The 1st month of the show had gone well, but Susan started having throat issues and was diagnosed with 'nodes' on her throat from the strain of singing so much. The only cure for this type of condition was refraining from using your voice, so a decision had to be made, and Susan decided to drop out of the show. A replacement would be needed immediately with someone who knew the show and could hit the ground running.

Celeste Holm was a perfect choice. She flew in and spent two days rehearsing with the cast to get familiar with the changes that were implemented before going on and knocking it out of the park. Susan had stayed to assist her in the transition with a big going away party thrown in her honor by the Hotel just before her departure. It was hard saying goodbye because we'd become so close, and we both promised to get together after the show closed. But it was never to happen. In 1972 a lung tumor was detected that had metastasized, and shortly afterward, Susan had a seizure and was diagnosed with brain cancer. On March 14th, 1975, she had another seizure and passed away at her home in Beverly Hill, CA. Of all the 'Mame's' I would eventually work with, Susan would always remain 'My Best Girl' above all the others. She was kind, thoughtful, caring, immensely talented, and adored by all who knew her. She'd worked her way into my heart and was truly one of a kind.

I was nervous about working with Celeste. She was very different from Susan and was much more demanding of everyone around her. It took several weeks before I would go on with her in the role of Patrick because the Producers wanted her to get comfortable with Shawn before throwing me into the mix. When I did finally go on with her, it was intense, but we worked well together. I later heard from a reliable source that she'd asked the show's Producer's why they hadn't cast me in the role to begin with, as she liked me much better than Shawn. Yikes!

Fryer, Carr, and Harris's grand experiment wasn't working. The change from Susan to Celeste was having an impact on ticket sales, and the overall response from potential audience members was: "If I wanted to see a Broadway show, I'd go to Broadway." So, after another month, the decision was made to close the show. Instead of 6 months, we ran for a little over four before we packed our bags and flew back to New York. I, for one, was relieved. There was so little for me to do there, and I was going stir crazy. Besides, "The booby show," there was one other treat I would repeatedly see while we were there. "WHERE EAGLES DARE" was playing downtown, and after I saw it the first time, I went back again, and again. "Broadsword calling Danny boy" became my call of choice whenever I went looking for Shawn. If you've never seen the film, I highly recommend seeking it out as it's an edge of your seat thriller that still holds up well today.

Side note: We didn't return to NY right away after the show closed. My father came out as we'd decided to take a week and make the trip to Los Angles. It would be a site seeing family vacation with a chance to reconnect. Loretta Swit had a girlfriend in LA who she wanted to visit and asked if she and her little dog could tag along. We agreed, and the four of us, plus our dog and hers, piled into the car for the ride west. It usually took about 4 hours to get from Vegas to LA, but we pulled a small U-Haul trailer behind us, so the trip ended up taking close to 9 hours! The trailer was full of stuff that we (and Loretta) had acquired during our time in Vegas, and the added weight was limiting our speed to about 45 MPH. There was also the needed stops every so often to let us and the dogs take a pee break. Once in LA, we dropped Loretta off at her friends and found a one-week rental apartment on Franklin Ave. in Hollywood where we could stay. It was a fun time, without drama, and it was where my Father taught me how to swim.

Personal Note: 1969 was my year of 'awakening.' I was 11 years old and had started identifying specific music and films that I would call my own. My father had often taken me to see James Bond double features in NY, but they'd all been released when I was younger before becoming 'aware' of their eventual impact on me. 1969 saw the release of "ON HER MAJESTY'S SECRET SERVICE," and I latched on to the franchise and composer John

Barry's score. Connery would always be the best Bond, but OHMSS became 'my' Bond film. My passion for film scores and favorite composers started here, and movies like "PLANET OF THE APES," "WHERE EAGLES DARE," "SILENT RUNNING," "ONCE UPON A TIME IN THE WEST," "FANTASTIC VOYAGE," "ROBINSON CRUSOE ON MARS," and many others would influence my taste in film and film scores. Over the years, I've become something of a film music enthusiast, amassing a sizable collection of soundtracks.

"MAME" Pt.3

Upon returning to Manhattan, Loretta Marshall had wasted no time getting me right back out to audition for several TV projects, both of which I booked. The first one was for a TV Special starring Dick Van Dyke and Carol Channing. Entitled "I'M A FAN," it was a one-hour variety show celebrating sports fans and their intense passion over their favorite pastimes. I was featured in two skits. In the first one, I played Dick and Carol's son, and in the other, I was a kid in a Little League team. The second booking was for me to be one of the kids that lived in the neighborhood of a little-known place called 'SESAME STREET". The new series was being produced by CTW (Children's Television Workshop) and launched on PBS stations all across America on November 10th, 1969. I appeared in episode #8, which aired on November 19th. Of course, no one at the time had any idea that SS would turn out to be such a huge success, or that two years later, I would find myself working for CTW again in another new series.

An interesting tidbit is what happened when Kermit the Frog first met Stephen 'Kermit' Gustafson. During the shoot, Jim Henson would play around with the kids via the Muppet characters he created for the show's launch. Big Bird was there as was Bert and Ernie, Grover and the Cookie Monster, but it was Kermit who Jim would use to interact with us kids in between takes. At one point, Kermit popped up just inside Mr. Hooper's store. I spotted him out of the corner of my eye and made my way over to see what he was doing. We started a dialog, and I quickly revealed to him that my middle name was also 'Kermit"! Jim ran with it, enticing many of the crew and others to join in watching the interchange between the Muppet and me. It was another one of those magic moments that I always seemed to be at the center of.

No sooner had I finished filming these two shows when Loretta received a phone call from Director John Bowab. There was a National tour of "Mame" Starring Sheila Smith already on the road, and the boy that was playing

Patrick Dennis was leaving the show. It seemed that his mother just couldn't handle the idea of being on tour for such an extended period and opted out of their contract. John was desperate. They were only in their 2nd week, with three months still to go, and he was losing his Patrick! Since I already knew the show, he pleaded with Loretta to book me and fly my Mother and me out to Texas, where they were currently performing. We all agreed it was the best solution, and the additional compensation I would receive for bailing them out wouldn't hurt either.

In less than 24 hours, my mother and I were on a flight to Texas that would arrive late in the evening, just around the time the shows evening performance was coming to a close. A limo picked us up at the airport, and we quickly made our way to the Theatre. The curtain had just come down, and John rushed me onto the stage to introduce me to the cast. Everyone would need to stay to do a quick run through as I would be going on the very next night! It was surreal.

We finished the 'pick-up' rehearsal around 1:00 am and then were taken to our hotel for a good night's rest. I went on later that night without a hitch. Everyone was impressed, and we spent the next three months touring the USA and cities on both sides of Canada. A tutor provided by the production handled the schoolwork, but it was the tour itself that provided the best education. We visited two major cities in every state, which allowed for plenty of site seeing. Museums, Parks, cultural landmarks, and other historical places of interest were available for a 1st hand look at our Countries history and heritage. Reading about history was one thing, but to actually be there up close, was far more impactful than words on a page. My education never suffered in the least and proved to be all the more enriching due to its 'hands-on' experience.

"MAME" Pt. 4

It was now June of 1970, and the tour was coming to a close. The summer shows were starting to gear up, and as fate would have it, John Bowab was directing yet another production of "Mame" for the same Guber-Gross circuit I'd done for the "THE MUSIC MAN." This time it was to be Patrice Munsel in the lead, and John wasted no time in booking me for the role once again. Patrice was a coloratura soprano and, at the age of 17, was the youngest singer to ever star at the Metropolitan Opera. After 225 performances between 1943 and 1958, Patrice retired from the Met and starred in numerous Musical Theatrical productions.

"MAME" With Patrice Munsel (Martini scene), 1970

Patrice was a doll and so easy to work with. The production was once again 'in-the-round,' so blocking and choreography would shift from a proscenium presentation to a circular one. This production even allowed me to work with my Aunt Hazel again, who was also a favorite of John's.

The show's run was pretty uneventful. It received excellent reviews, but I don't remember very many details about it as my time doing "MAME" had all started to become a blur. Patrice would become the 8th actress I'd work with performing the role of Mame. My over 400 performances in the show would include Janice Paige, Patrice Munsel, Susan Hayward, Celeste Holme, Sheila Smith, Anne Russel, and several others who'd been understudies. To this day, I still hold the record for having worked with more 'Mame's' and done more performances the any other Patrick Dennis in the business.

"A THOUSAND CLOWNS"

"MAME" closed in early September of 1970, and for the first time in quite a while, I didn't have any bookings. I managed to shoot a few more commercials but, those were day jobs, so mother and I were finally able to come 'Home' to Newington and spend the Christmas Holiday with my father and grandparents. The season was memorable, but I was having some problems with anxiety, as I'd gotten used to either being on the road or living in NY city where life was happening 24 hours a day. The 'quiet' of the rural setting was in stark contrast to the constant excitement of traveling to new places and always being at the center of things. I began to have what is described today as 'Panic attacks. Back then, when children exhibited signs like this, it was brushed off as 'hyper-active' behavior. My mother talked to the Doctor who prescribed Diazepam as a means of calming me down, but the side effects were proving troublesome, so I eventually stopped taking it. The only real solution for my 'condition' was to limit my time in Connecticut and stay in Manhattan whenever possible. The needed sensory stimulation created by the sounds of the city had become comforting and offered relief from the 'silence' induced panic of nights spent in New England.

Just after the first of the year in 1971, I was offered the role of Nick Burns in Herb Gardner's "A THOUSAND CLOWNS" to be staged at Theatre West in Springfield, Massachusetts. Theatre West was a professional venue that had a resident company of adult actors, but no kids. My reputation as a child actor and the fact that I was a Hartford native brought me to their attention. So, it was an easy decision for them to cast me.

"A THOUSAND CLOWNS" 1971

My Agent approved and thought it would be both another 'feather in my cap' and provide me with time in Connecticut to help get my anxieties under control.

The show starred (besides me) Jerry Hardin and Leon B. Stevens. Jerry had a stable career in NY, and Leon was a native of Manchester, New Hampshire. Jerry also had a 4-year-old daughter named Melora, who later went on to a successful acting career of her own starting in 1977.

"A THOUSAND CLOWNS" 1971

The first read-through happened the last week in January with an opening night scheduled for March 12th, and it would be a night I would not soon forget. I was still struggling with anxiety issues due to our staying at our home in Newington as it was reasonably close to the Theatre in Springfield. Up till then, I'd never had stage fright or a case of nerves about performing, but in this instance, the anxiety and panic I felt were overwhelming. Just moments before the show started, I threw up backstage. I was shaking and crying, so the stage manager held off the start time for about five minutes as my mother helped me clean up and compose myself. Just a few encouraging words from her seemed to do the trick, and I pulled it together enough to go on. It was the first and only time that ever happened, but it was a wake-up call to everyone around me that 'the perfect little man' was starting to buckle under the stress of it all.

"A THOUSAND CLOWNS" With Leon B. Stevens, 1971

"Clowns" had a solid six-week run and received excellent reviews. And Except for the opening night incident, I had a great time doing this show. It was my first full comedy outing, and I seemed to have a knack for the genre's needed timing and delivery that I didn't know I had. I loved hearing the audience respond to my performance and came out of the experience with a newfound confidence that would serve me well for what was to come.

"THE ELECTRIC COMPANY"

The unprecedented success of "SESAME STREET" made a follow-up series inevitable. "SS" was geared for toddlers and children up to about eight years of age, so the new show would put its focus on kids from 7-10-years-old that had learned the alphabet and were now ready to focus on grammar and reading skills. CTW (Children's Television Workshop), who were the creative geniuses behind "SS," called the program "THE ELECTRIC COMPANY." Paul Dooley was the show's creator and head writer, which is why the show featured slightly more mature humor that ofttimes found itself sailing over the heads of its intended audience. The kids might not pick up on it, but it resonated with the Parents who became fond of watching the show right along with their offspring.

TEC Season One

The 1st season of "TEC" starred a cast of well-known and not so well-known performers. Bill Cosby and Rita Moreno checked off the well-known box with Judy Graubart, Lee Chamberlin, and Skip Hinnant filling in the not-so-well-known box. The one additional lead cast member who was not yet familiar to audiences was Morgan Freeman. Morgan was still a few years away from starting his ascent towards becoming the legendary icon he is today. The secondary cast consisted of 5 kids who made up the rock band known as the 'Short Circus.' Along with myself on Drums, there was Melanie Henderson ("THE ME NOBODY KNOWS") on Guitar, June Angela ("THE KING AND I" revivals), Vocals/Tambourine, Douglas Grant ("THE LANDLORD") "bass Guitar" and Irene Cara ("FAME") Vocals/Tambourine. Irene, of course, would go on to become a singing sensation with many big hits during her illustrious career.

The audition process was arduous. CTW had held casting calls in NY, Los Angeles, and several other major cities to find kids who could sing, dance, act and play their own instruments. I had a total of five auditions before finally landing my role. An interesting fact regarding our character names was that each of us had the honor of picking it ourselves. I picked mine (Buddy) because I admired drummer 'Buddy' Rich, June picked hers (Julie) to honor Julie Andrews, and Melanie chose to let the writers decide (Kathy). Douglas was known as (Zach) and Irene chose (Iris) for reasons I don't recall. It was at that point that the "Short Circus" was officially born. One of our first songs on the show served as an introduction to our characters with Melanie, June, and I, singing about our name and the things we liked to do. 'My name is Buddy,' has stuck with me ever since, along with my now infamous bathtub song, "I wish I didn't Have to Wash."

The first season was shot at a studio on Manhattan's Eastside before moving to Reeves TeleTape Studios at Broadway and 81st St for the remainder of filming, and I'll never forget that 1st day. The Short Circus members had already met each other during casting because our 'chemistry' together was an essential part of creating the group. Now it was time for us to meet the

Adult cast members, which was very exciting. I was an enormous fan of Bill Cosby's comedy albums and had watched him on "I Spy" with Robert Culp. I knew practically all of his routines by heart and couldn't wait to meet him. When I spotted him sitting alone on the set, I walked over and introduced myself. He was very cordial and shook my hand. I told him, "I have all your albums," to which he responded, "Give'em back." It was classic Cosby and not at all the response I was expecting! He was quick-witted and often had the cast in stitches with his shenanigans both on and behind the sets.

Our Apartment was located on 1st Ave between 50th and 51st Streets, an area known as Beekman Place. It was strictly a coincidence that Beekman Place was also the location of Mame Dennis' home in the play! With production moving uptown and to the Westside, we decided to move to larger quarters but still stay on the Eastside. We ended up in a new building on 81st St. and 1st Ave, in a section of Manhattan known as Yorkville. Geographically all I had to do was grab the bus at the corner of 79th and 1^{st,} and it would take me straight through Central Park to Broadway and 79th. A two-block walk from there, and I was at TeleTape on 81st. It was around this time that I also ended up doing a bunch of voice over (dubbing) work at TITRA Sound located on Broadway. One project I lent my voice to was a Japanese Anime import called "Marine Boy." The term 'Anime' didn't yet exist, and cartoons back then were just referred to as animation. 'MARINE BOY' led to work on 'SPEED RACER' and 'KIMBA THE WHITE LION.' It was also at TITRA that I did the dubbing for the Swedish Import of Astrid Lindgren's "Pippi Longstockings" film series. I was the voice of 'Tommy' in the English dubbed version of "PIPPI IN THE SOUTH SEAS."

TEC was slated to premiere on PBS October 25th, 1971, but in many areas, a preview, "Here comes The Electric Company," was aired in syndication through the Sponsor 'Johnson Wax.' The show became another instant hit for CTW with the "Short Circus" becoming a fan favorite. During its run, the show received numerous awards, including an Emmy and a Grammy for Best Children's program and Best Children's Album of the year in 1973. As cast members, we were given 'Honorary' awards status in both instances from each of the respective Guilds.

Side Note: *Working with Cosby proved challenging. You never knew what sort of mood he was in on any given day and found yourself asking someone on set what the 'Cos' Temp was when you got there. Bill could either be friendly and playful or short-tempered and quick to snap. In my opinion, his frustration over not yet being the 'superstar' he saw himself as was eating away at him, and he felt that a PBS show like TEC wasn't going to help him get there. He departed the show at the end of season 1 to move on to bigger and better things. Luis Avalos joined the cast for season 2, and Jim Boyd, who was strictly an off-camera voice actor and puppeteer during the first season, began appearing on-camera in the second season, mostly in the role of J. Arthur Crank. Season 3 also saw Hattie Winston replace Lee Chamberlain, who, like Cosby, had decided to leave for career growth.*

TEC 'Short Circus' Season Two

With season 2 getting ready to start filming, we were informed that Irene Cara also would not be returning. She wanted to focus on her singing career, so a replacement would be needed to fill her spot. The Producers had the good judgment to ask us kids if we knew anybody who might be right for the part, and I immediately thought of Denise Nickerson, who I'd worked with in "THE MUSIC MAN." The call went out, and her audition was scheduled, with the producers having us participate in making sure her chemistry jived with ours. Denise was a natural and landed her role, who she named 'Allison.' It was now 1972, and filming this season was a blast. The original four of us all had time to bond as a group, and adding Denise (for me) just made things even more comfortable. The songs and skits had also become more plentiful for us due to our growing popularity, and a TEC cast album was created that included many of our best-known favorites.

Side Note: 1972 also saw me and June Angela perform in the Milliken Breakfast Show at the Waldorf Astoria. The Milliken Company was a large Textile manufacturer with much of their product used in clothing. From 1956 to 1980, they would produce a Broadway-level Musical Production that featured costumes made from the various materials they manufactured. I played the role of 'The Kid' opposite such luminaries as Lou Jacobi, Chita Rivera, Arnold Stang, Madeline Kahn, and Fred Travalena. One big plus in doing this show was that you got to keep your entire tailor-made wardrobe after the show closed!

When season three of TEC rolled around, and for reasons I'm not real clear about, both Douglas and Denise left the show. Once again, the Producers reached out to us for input. I was sorry to see them go, but I knew Denise's career was gaining forward momentum on other fronts, so I wasn't worried about her future. As the only two boys in the group, Douglas and I had become close and often got together outside of filming to 'jam' on music that was more sophisticated then what we did on the show. 'Yes,' 'King Crimson' and 'Jimi Hendrix' were just a few of the influencers we tried to emulate. Douglas's presence was sorely missed, but his replacement would end up being another friend of both mine and June's from Dance class! Since I'd first signed with Marshall Management, dance class was a necessary evil for any child actor hoping to make it in NY. Back then, it wasn't enough to just 'act.' You had to be proficient in all areas of performing, as you never knew when you would be called upon to sing or dance at a moment's notice. If you couldn't deliver, then your chances of succeeding were slim to none.

The Phil Black Dance Studio was famous in NY for attracting the best dancers from Broadway and elsewhere to train under Phil's tutelage. I went on a semi-regular basis, but to be honest, I utterly hated going and would sometimes fight tooth and nail with my Mother to avoid it. I could dance well, but Phil always pushed his students harder and harder to improve even if he knew they would never become a 'great' dancer. It was often humiliating when he would single you out and force you to the front of the class, so everyone could see what NOT to do. Despite his talent and ability to produce amazing Broadway dancers, I sometimes felt his style was abusive. Over the years, I realized it was mostly my not wanting to go rather than anything Phil did to push his students to excel.

Be that as it may, one of the best things to come out of my time in class was a friendship with a young dancer named Gregg Burge. Gregg was born to dance. The dance studio could be filled with top-notch dancers, and your eye would always end up on Gregg. At sixteen-years-old Gregg had already surpassed most of the best dancers in town. June Angela was a regular attendee at Phil's and was also friends with Gregg, so we both blurted out his name at the same time when the TEC producers asked for a recommendation. As with Denise, Gregg was brought in for a tryout, and it was immediately apparent that he was a good fit. Next came a Broadway darling named Bayn Johnson who had come to their attention via her turn in off- Broadway's "CURLEY MCDIMPLE" opposite Bernadette Peters. Bayn had an infectious energy, and we took to her instantly. The season three Short Circus was now complete, and our dancing duties were in good hands with Choreographer Patricia Birch at the helm. (FYI) Gregg would later play the role of 'Richie' in the 1985 film version of "A Chorus Line," and serve as assistant Choreographer alongside Jeffrey Horniday. Gregg passed away at the age of 40 on July 4th, 1998, from a brain tumor. Broadway and the world lost one of its most shining talents on that day.

TEC AT LINCOLN CENTER: 1973 My Solo!

Side Note: During the first two seasons, all of the 'Short Circus's' performing on the show had been confined to taping in the studio or pre-recording songs in smaller studios elsewhere in town. In 73' the new 'Short Circus' stepped out onto the stage at Lincoln Center for three live performances that showcased all our best-known songs. We would later perform the show again at Reverend Jesse Jackson's 1973 PUSH Expo in Chicago, where over 40,000 people would watch us live!

TEC AT LINCOLN CENTER: 1973

"GET HAPPY"

TEC shot all their episodes at one time over a four to six-month period, which left me the remaining months to pursue other prospects. Commercials were a given, and I was still booking a few of those from time to time, but two other terrific opportunities arose after we wrapped season three. The first was something truly special. A Television Variety Special called "GET HAPPY," which was a salute to the music of Harold Arlen. Arlen and his composing partner, Yip Harburg (Lyricist), were responsible for all the songs in "THE WIZARD OF OZ" and tons of other hits from the '30s to the '60s. This show would have one of the most star-studded casts I'd ever work with outside of "OUR TOWN." The show's concept had Jack Lemmon making his way along a yellow brick road where he came across various performers to share one of Arlen's famous hits with. Johnny Mathis, Diahann Carrol, Doc Severinsen, and 'Mama' Cass Elliot all had their moment with Jack, and so did I.

"GET HAPPY" Me & Jack, 1973

Mid-way through the show, Jack stops at Kool-Aide stand for a cold drink. When he sits down, I appear as "Joe," the bartender, a kid in colorful overalls with a beanie cap on his head. We exchange a bit of dialog before he notices a hand-drawn clock on the bar that indicates it's 'A Quarter to Three,' another of Arlen's famous melodies. Jack starts to sing the familiar lyrics and then breaks into a soft shoe routine. I jump in to join him, and the two of us dance to the remainder of the music before he heads back off down the Yellow brick road. It was magical.

"GET HAPPY" With Jack Lemmon, Cass Elliot, Johnny Mathis, Diahann Carrol, & Doc Severinsen 1973

Except for Doc Severinsen, who I'd worked with before, when The Short Circus performed on the Tonight Show in 1971, the rest of the cast were legends in my eyes. Mathis and Mama Cass were two of the most wonderful people I'd ever had the pleasure to work with. Dianne Carrol was pleasant but reserved, and Jack Lemmon was …. well, Jack Lemmon. He was funny, professional, approachable, and always entertaining to watch work. The time I spent with him was probably the most gratifying experience I had throughout my entire performing career.

Rehearsals took place in New York for a week before we flew to Ontario, Canada, for the shoot. An Ontario studio was picked for filming as the tax breaks in Canada made it more beneficial for the producers. What it didn't do was make things easier for the cast and crew. It was the middle of winter in Ontario, and the snow was falling so thick you could barely see a foot in front of your face. The Studio was about an hour's drive from the hotel where we stayed, but it wound up taking closer to two to get there because of the weather. My segment with Jack was scheduled to film at around 11:00 am on the 2nd day of shooting, so my Mother and I grabbed a shuttle van at 8:00 am to make sure we got there for my 10:am call time. The snowfall had subsided, making things a bit more pleasant, and the ride there took less time than we had anticipated.

As soon as we arrived, I made my way to wardrobe to get dressed and then makeup. Once I was done, I went to the soundstage to check in with the AD (assistant director) and let him know I was ready. 11:00 am rolled on by along with Noon, 1:00 pm, 2:00 pm, and Three o'clock. I kept checking, but he assured me it would be soon. They were having some technical issues, and some retakes had been necessary. I was used to delays and sitting for hours on sets and didn't think it was out of the ordinary, so I went back to waiting and rehearsing my steps on my own. 7:00 pm rolled around, and I was still waiting. My mom had finished both the books she'd brought with her and decided it would be Okay to head back to the Hotel. I was used to handling things independently, and she knew that the crew would take good care of me and get me back safely. Now, remember, this 1973 and child labor laws were not what they are today, so this type of lengthy delay would never be allowed to happen now.

It was 9:00 pm by the time the AD came and said they were ready for me. I'd been napping for the last 90 mins and was rejuvenated and raring to go. Surprisingly, Jack looked none the worse for wear despite the long hours he'd been working while I'd been waiting. We did a quick run-through for the cameras, and then tape was rolling. A few hours later, the Director yelled 'That's a wrap… for tonight," and I hustled it back to my dressing room so I could change and catch the last Van back to the Hotel.

The last van had already left at 11:00 pm. With Jack and I, the only two performers remaining and Jack having his own Limo, nobody thought to alert the van driver to wait for me! I stepped outside the stage door to find myself standing in near dark, with only a small light illuminating the space just under the stage door. The snow was falling again, and the temperature was probably about 20 degrees. Just as I began to panic and turned to go back in, a set of headlights came around the corner, and Jack's Limo pulled up. The back window opened, and Jack poked his head out and said, "Get in here, it's too damn cold." I didn't hesitate and ran around to the other side, where the driver held the door open for me. I climbed in and thanked Jack for picking me up, telling him how relieved I was. For the next two hours, I was in seventh heaven.

Jack Lemmon, like Charlton Heston, had a body of work that was truly impressive. There was "MISTER ROBERTS" for which he won the Academy Award, "SOME LIKE IT HOT," "THE APARTMENT," "DAYS OF WINE AND ROSES," "THE ODD COUPLE," "THE-OUT-OF-TOWNERS," and many more. I could have chosen any one of them to ask questions about, but the one film I absolutely had to discuss was "THE GREAT RACE." Like "PLANET OF THE APES," "RACE" was my favorite film, and here I was locked in a limo with the one and only 'Professor Fate'!

As with Heston, Jack was kind, patient, and more than willing to delight me with stories of what shooting the picture was like. I was the proverbial 'kid in a candy store' listening to him share anecdotes about Tony Curtis and Natalie Wood and some of the behind the scenes shenanigans that went on. I didn't want it to end, but we eventually arrived back at the Hotel and had to part company. Not very many people are fortunate enough to engage one on one with their favorite performers in private settings such as a limo or a booth in a coffee shop. I'd had the good fortune to be given both of those with two of my biggest idols. All I needed now was to work with Sean Connery, and my list would be complete!

VARIETY Announcement, 1973

"Get Happy" aired on Sunday, February 25th, 1973, on NBC and was a delightful hour of song and dance that I'm proud to have been associated with. I wish it were possible to view again today, but according to the NBC archives, it no longer exists. As with many 'taped' programs from the era, many shows have simply been lost or destroyed. The same is true for "I'm A Fan" and many other taped productions I'd done. Only their memories have survived.

Side note: *Many years later, around 1999, I had the good fortune of running into Johnny Mathis at Dave's 'The Laser place' in Studio City, CA. Dave's was a laserdisc and high-end audio/visual retailer at the time, which I often frequented. On one occasion, I spotted Johnny browsing the aisles and approached him. I wasn't sure he would remember me or even be receptive enough to engage in conversation, but he allowed me to re-introduce myself and remind him of our time together in NY and Canada. He beamed and immediately asked me how my Mother was and what I'd been doing all these years. We stood there speaking for about 15 minutes before going our separate ways, and I couldn't help but think how blessed I'd been to have worked with such amazing people over the years. Johnny truly is an American treasure.*

"ROOKIE OF THE YEAR"

The next opportunity I had afforded me the chance to play opposite Jodie Foster in the 2nd season opener of the daytime series "The ABC Afterschool Special." The episode's title was "ROOKIE OF THE YEAR" and was based on the book "Not bad for a Girl." Jodie played 'Sharon,' an eleven-year-old who joins her brother's little league team much to the irritation of the all-male players. I played 'Ralph,' the most vocal of the ballplayers and Sharon's biggest anti-advocate.

"Rookie" was shot in Upstate in NY during one of the hottest summers on record. The heat and humidity were off the charts, and we'd often joke about how many barrels of sweat we must be producing daily. It was brutal but fun.

I was 4 years older than Jodie at the time but was playing younger. Even at 15, I still looked 11, so we matched up pretty well, but what I remember most about the shoot was how focused Jodie was even back then. We could be swimming and having fun in the pool at the Hotel playing 'Marco Polo' one minute, and then on set the next where she became all business. All the other kids were always rowdy and joking around between takes but not Jodie. It was clear to me then that she would be a force to be reckoned with as her career moved forward.

Our moms became friends during the shoot, and a little over a year later, after we moved to LA, Brandy (Jodie's mom) and my mom rekindled their friendship. Brandy was even going out of her way to get Disney interested in me for some upcoming projects Jodie was slated to appear in!

'ROOKIE' aired on ABC on October 3rd, 1973, and was well received. It even won the Daytime Emmy for Outstanding Entertainment Children's Special of that year. Five years later, at the age of twenty, I would end up doing another After School Special called "THE RAG TAG CHAMPS" with Larry B. Scott ("A HERO AIN'T NOTHIN BUT A SANDWICH," "SPACE CAMP").

"TEC" MY FINAL SEASON

There had been some rumored discussion early on in the show's 1st season that the members of the Short Circus would eventually (as the grew up) become a part of the Adult cast with new kids filling in their spots. But it proved to be just a rumor and nothing more. I'd gone through a 'natural life occurrence' called puberty during season 3, which caused my voice to dip and change the sound of our harmonies. June and I had always handled the high parts, but now I could no longer hit the needed notes, as written by the show's principal composer Joe Raposo. I was also starting to grow in height and experience other physical changes, so Season 4 would be my last along with Gregg, Melanie, and Bayn. June Angela was the only original member of the group who remained, with the rest of us replaced by Janina Mathews (Gail), Réjane Magloire (Samantha), Rodney Lewis (Charlie), and Todd Graff (Jesse). The show lasted only two more seasons after we left before being canceled in 1977 at the height of its popularity. Unlike its counterpart *Sesame Street,* which licensed its Muppet characters for merchandising, *TEC* never had a stand-alone brand or marketable character that could generate additional profits. A partnership with Marvel Comics attempted to infuse new life into the series by introducing Spiderman (Spidey Super Stories). Still, the PBS stations and statewide networks that aired the show often complained that Children's Television Workshop "soaked up too much money in public television." The stations demanded that one of the programs, either Sesame Street or TEC, be put into reruns to save money. Since Sesame Street was the cash cow juggernaut, TEC got the ax.

"SPIDEY SUPER STORIES" 1974

Side Note: A by-product of being seen on TV every day made for a fair amount of difficulty when I was in public. The parents, not so much the kids, would recognize me and ask for autographs, often generating a crowd around me on the street that would grow as more people realized who I was. There was one time when I was at Radio City Music Hall just minding myself and taking in a movie when, in the dark of the theatre, I felt a tug on my left sleeve. I was sitting on the aisle and turned to see three mothers kneeling next to me, desperately wanting my autograph for their kids. I obliged, as I always did, but honestly just wanted to be left alone so I could watch the movie.

That year I also attended the Ringling Bros. Barnum and Bailey Circus at Madison Square Garden. While sitting in the risers taking in the show, I received a tap on my shoulder from behind. I turned to see a young girl of about 12 hand me a pad and ask if she could have my autograph. I said "sure," signed the note pad, and handed it back.... which she, in turn, handed back to me and said, "we all want one." I spun around in my seat to see an entire Girl Scout Troop of about 25 young ladies all smiling and swooning over receiving my signature. Never one to deny my fans, I spent the next 30 mins trying to watch the show and scribble away on the pad to satisfy the request. But here's the kicker. Little did I know that while watching one of the female Aerial Trapeze flyers in the center ring, I was actually watching...now get this... my future wife to be 23 years later in 1997!

I remember my last season being bittersweet. We did some great work and were still having fun, but knowing our days were numbered proved to be a drag (very 70's lingo). By now, my father had left his law enforcement position as Sergeant and had become the General Manager of a Bar/Café called THE OFFICE. The running joke was that a husband could phone his wife at the end of the workday and tell her he would be late at 'the office". It was a clever marketing ploy that worked. The Pub was always busy with my father often having to tend bar to meet the demands. Things were still strained between my parents, but they'd resigned themselves to staying together and keeping things low key for my sake. They only wanted the best for me and didn't want to add more stress to my already demanding career.

Every year at Lincoln Square Academy, we'd put on a 'Talent Show.' With nearly all the student's in the business, the participants offered up a topflight variety show of singing, dancing, and comedy, the likes of which could only be found on a Broadway stage. Well, in 1974, before I turned 16 and we left NY for LA, that's precisely what the Academy did. My former "OUR TOWN" Theatre 'The ANTA' was rented by LSA for a week and sold tickets for a 'Student Review' of industry kids doing what they did best.... perform. I did a PG-rated rendition of a George Carlin routine, Robby Benson ("ONE ON ONE" "ICE CASTLES") played the guitar and sang, and young members of Alvin Ailey's Dance Theatre of Harlem performed along with a whole bunch of other students showcasing their talents. Demand for tickets to see the show exceeded the run's limit, so additional afternoon performances were added to meet the requests. It ended up being a one-time thing and never happened again.

ACT TWO: HURRAY FOR HOLLYWOOD

By this time in 1974, I'd pretty much done all I could do regarding Stage, Television, and Commercial work in NY. The next logical step was to see what Hollywood would have to offer through Episodic TV and Feature Films. My Father agreed to come along and see what work he could find in LA, while I secured an Agent and hopefully started booking some jobs. I was also going to have to continue my schooling via correspondence from LSA.

We relinquished our apartments in NY and CT., loaded up a big U-Haul, and made the trek across the country to the city of Angels. The ride was long but uneventful, and upon our arrival, we were fortunate to find a spiffy 'penthouse' like apartment on Miller Dr. at Sunset Blvd. and La Cienega. The apartment complex was small, with only about 16 units in total. It sat on a hill, so when you entered at Street level, you had to walk up to get to the pool level. Several sets of stairs above that and overlooking the pool was our unit. It was classic Hollywood. We got settled in, and a few weeks later, I celebrated my 16th birthday. It was an event that the whole complex participated in, ending with my being unceremoniously tossed into the pool.

The school year was about to start, and I'd been provided with a packet of lessons and reading assignments from LSA before we'd left. At 16, I was already behind. I'd just barely managed to graduate Jr. High School from LSA in a ceremony held at Lincoln Center, but I would soon lose the time I should have been a Freshman and a bit of the time, I should have been a Sophomore in High school. I got started on the correspondence but quickly let it slide. I was a 16-year-old in Hollywood. There was too much to see and do to keep me from burying my face in schoolwork.

Snagging an agent didn't take long with the help of Jodie Foster's Mom Brandy, and I wound up signing with the 'Toni Kelman Agency," who was also Jodie's Agent. Toni was to Hollywood what Loretta Marshall was to NY. She was one of the top children and young adult agents in LA and handled clients like Jodie, Willie Aames, Larry Wilcox, Lance Kerwin, Michael Baldwin, Maureen McCormick, and Susan Olsen. At one point, she even represented a very young Stacy Ann Ferguson who, many years later, would go on to become 'Fergie of 'The Black-Eyed Peas'! All of Toni's kids worked, and it didn't take me long to book my first show. I was something of a novelty in LA. I was a NY actor with extensive stage experience that none of the LA kids had, and the casting directors took notice.

One of my very first LA auditions was on the Paramount lot, and for the life of me, I can't remember what it was for. What I do remember was meeting another young man there who would become one of my best friends for years to come. Michael Blake was also auditioning, and we struck up a conversation while waiting to read. Michael's Father was Larry J. Blake, a long-time character actor who'd played the Bartender in "HIGH NOON" with Gary Cooper. Michael was also an aficionado of everything related to the life and career of Lon Chaney. He was obsessed with make-up and the remarkable characters that Chaney had created with its use. Michael would later become an Emmy award-winning makeup artist in his own right and publish several books that chronicled Chaney's life and career. Mike was to become the 2nd member of a 3-man team dubbed "The Musketeers." Mike and I were the 1st two, and the 3rd fellow, who joined us a bit later, was Terry Lamfers. Terry worked at Universal Studios in a department known as 'Central Files.' It was a large warehouse on the lot where all the records and documentation generated by the studio were housed for reference. Remember, this was long before computers existed, so you can imagine the difficulty in trying to log and keep track of hundreds of thousands of items that dated back to the studios beginning! The three of us became inseparable and would share many adventures, but more on that later.

"SHAZAM"

"SHAZAM" was a Saturday morning kids show loosely based on the comic book adventures of young Billy Batson (aka 'Shazam') and his Mentor. It starred Michael Gray as Billy Batson, Les Tremayne as the Mentor, and Barry Bostwick as Billy's alter ego 'Shazam.' It was in its first season of filming, and I landed the 'Problem Kid' of the week guest star role. It was episode 13, entitled: "THE BRAGGART," where I played a boy named ALAN who lies to impress his friends and ends up putting all of them in danger because of it. 'Always tell the truth' was the moral of the story.

The episode was filmed in and around the Studio City area of the Valley and at the Griffith Park Zoo. The Zoo was where all the 'action' took place as my character had to prove one of his lies and enter the cage of a wild animal. I first entered the enclosure of a sizeable cinereous vulture that gets spooked and flies out of its cage. My friends and I chase after it, and it lands inside the Lion pen. I climb over the fence and into the pen, where a large Lion confronts me. It takes "Shazam" to appear on the scene at the last minute and wrestle the Lion to save the day."THE BRAGGART" aired on CBS November 30th, 1974, and it looked like I was finally on my way to establishing a new career in Hollywood.

On the heels of "SHAZAM" came a small role in a TV movie called "SARAH T-PORTRAIT OF A TEENAGE ALCOHOLIC." It starred Linda Blair ("THE EXORCIST") and a pre-STAR WARS, Mark Hamill. Oh, and it was directed by none other than Richard Donner, who'd go on to direct ("SUPERMAN") in 1978.

I was making progress, but my schooling needed to resume asap, so Toni recommended I enroll at the 'Hollywood Professional School.' Like LSA in NY, the HPS curriculum was formulated to accommodate High School age performers working in Los Angeles. Lance Kerwin went there, and so did Mackenzie Phillips ("ONE DAY AT A TIME"). Even Andy Williams's nephews (the twins) went there. The School was located in the heart of Hollywood near Hollywood Blvd and Western Ave, making it easy to get to casting offices and locations. There was only one class per grade level, and the day was split in half between morning and afternoon school. The morning school went from 8:00 am to 12:30 pm and the afternoon school went from 1:30 pm to 5:00 pm. You could choose either one or both depending on your needs. As I was already two years behind my age group, I ended up doing both to catch up. I was able to skip my Freshman year and focus on being a Sophomore for one year, followed by one semester as a Junior and the last semester as a Senior. This revised plan allowed me to graduate with my proper age group just before turning eighteen. It was a grueling two years of pounding the books, but I ended up with an 'A' average despite squeezing in appearances on "CHIPS," "JAMES AT 16," and a PBS Movie called "THE GOLD WATCH" starring Mako ("THE SAND PEBBLES," "PACIFIC OVERTURES") and Soon-Tek Oh ("THE MAN WITH THE GOLDEN GUN," "THE FINAL COUNTDOWN")

We'd stayed on Miller Drive for about a year before moving into a newer, larger apartment on Alta Loma Road just below Sunset and adjacent to the famous 'Playboy' building. We had a top floor corner unit that overlooked the pool and tennis court directly below. We fudged my age to 18 to rent there as they had a NO CHILDREN policy. Of course, everyone in the building new I was only 16, but nobody cared. I was ahead of my years and in no way a troublemaker. My father had secured a position working for the MTA (Mass Transit Authority) in El Monte as a Security Supervisor. It was a bit of a drive, but he didn't seem to mind. He kept regular daytime hours, which allowed him to be home by dinner time, but he had also fallen prey to Hollywood's social enticements and would spend many of his off-hours at any one of the famous bars on the Sunset strip. It didn't take long before the yelling and tears started again between him and my mother.

WITNESS TO MURDER:

On the night of February 12th, 1976, I witnessed the murder of Actor Sal Mineo. His apartment complex was adjacent to ours on the corner of Holloway Dr. and Alta Loma Road, and there was a driveway that ran between the two buildings. I was walking my dog along the side of our complex that was slightly elevated from the intersecting driveway due to the downward slope of the Street. I watched a car come up the driveway and turn into a carport located underneath the apartments down and across from me. A man got out and proceeded to enter a narrow walkway that led to the apartment's courtyard. A moment later, I heard the man screaming, "No, no…get away from me!" as he came backing out of the walkway. Another man in dark clothes with light curly hair emerged and then plowed into him, knocking him down as he passed. Sal hit the pavement screaming for help as a wash of blood came pouring out onto the driveway. Several tenants poked their heads out their windows above him, and someone came out and rushed to Sal, trying to stop the flow of blood but was unsuccessful. I immediately ran back into my building with my dog and went upstairs to tell my folks what I'd just seen. I told my Father that I should go back down and inform the Police and Sheriff's officers what had happened.

As a former Police Officer himself, he'd been involved in many investigations and knew what was likely to happen if I got involved. He told me that "If you do this, you need to be prepared to follow it through to the end. As a witness, the investigating Detectives will not leave you alone until the case is solved. Can you handle that? Can you make that kind of commitment?" In hindsight, I should have taken his advice and said "No.," but I was so distraught over what'd happened that I said yes and then hurried back downstairs to see what was happening.

The crime scene was a wash of activity with both LAPD and Sheriff units filling the driveway along with an ambulance and a paramedic crews. The flashing emergency lights from all the vehicles cast an eerie glow over the scene as I tried to identify someone I could speak to. I finally spotted a Sheriff who was standing by his car, taking notes, and approached him. I told him that I had witnessed the altercation and wanted to provide them with my eyewitness account. The Sheriff immediately summoned an associate who pulled me aside to take my statement. After about 5 minutes of relaying the details, I suddenly found myself being unceremoniously escorted to the back of the car and told to get in. They opened the door and ushered me in the back seat. The officer said, "Just stay here until I come back." Now, keep in mind that at 16 years old, I was still a 'minor' and entitled to certain rights. Rights that were now on the verge of being violated. I spotted my Father coming out the side of our building but couldn't get his attention to let him know where I was. As he tried to find me in all the chaos, the car I was in started up and proceeded to leave the scene. I asked the officer behind the wheel where we were going, "The Station." was all that he said and then refused to answer any more of my questions.

The West Hollywood Sheriff's Station was very close by on the corner of San Vicente and Santa Monica Blvd, and we arrived there in less than 5 minutes. I was taken out of the car and led inside, where I was put in a small room and told to write down what I had seen on some paper that the officer handed to me. Just as I started to write, I could hear my father yelling at the night desk officer located at the station entrance. 'Where is my son! He's a minor, and you can't hold him without a parent present!" His yelling continued for another minute or so before they reluctantly brought him back to where I was sitting composing my statement. "Do not speak to each other." The officer said. "No discussion, just continue to write." Neither of us had any idea who'd been murdered and were never aware that 'Sal Mineo' had lived next door to us. It was only after the Detectives arrived two hours later that my Dad and I were informed of the victim's identity. It came as a real shock, leaving us both in a state of disbelief.

The time was now 2:00 am, and we were only just beginning the Q&A with the detectives. I was supposed to be at school in 6 hours, but the questioning went on until close to 5:00 am, so there was no way I would be attending classes that day. When we finished, the Detectives told us that due to the 'high profile' nature of the case and the fact that the assailant was still on the loose, Police protection would be necessary. "It's possible he might have seen you." Said one of the men. "He might decide to eliminate any witnesses, so a squad car will be assigned to you 24/7 until we're sure it's safe." I looked at my Father and said, "You were right. I should have thought this through before deciding to get involved." For the next six weeks, there was a police unit present everywhere I went. Outside our apartment, outside my school, anyplace I went, they went. It was irritating as hell, but it did provide a sense of safety, especially when knowing that whoever had killed Sal was still at large.

Just as my father had predicted, the Detectives called day and night hoping that I might have recalled some small detail that I hadn't relayed to them the night of the incident. They even went so far as to have me put under hypnosis to see if anything was hiding in my subconscious, some tidbit of information that would help them better identify the killer. It was a waste of time. I didn't provide any additional details other than what I'd already given them.

It would take nearly four years before 'Lionel Ray Williams' would be formally charged with Mineo's murder and ten counts of Robbery. I was called to testify before the grand jury in Downtown LA in February of 1979. Considerable confusion existed as to what witnesses had seen the night Mineo was murdered, and even I admitted to not having seen enough of Williams's face to identify whether he was black or white. Corrections officers later said they'd overheard Williams admit to the stabbing, with Williams' wife soon after confirming that on the night Mineo died, her husband had come home with blood on his shirt. Williams was found guilty and sentenced to 57 years in prison.

THE SARATOGA

I'd graduated High School in June of 1976 and now needed to decide if College was on the horizon. My mother felt that having a degree would be invaluable if I ever left the entertainment industry and took another type of work. I found the idea humorous and could only laugh at the thought of doing something other than acting as it had been my whole life up till then. Everything else paled by comparison. I'd been earning good money since I was eight years old and, during the TEC years, was one of the highest-paid child actors in NY at the time. Why would I even think of doing something else? Well, as it turned out, most of my High school pals were going in the fall, so I enrolled in some Film and Television classes at Los Angeles Valley College in North Hollywood just to be able to hang with my friends. It didn't take long for me to realize that I knew more about filmmaking than the instructors did and dropped out before completing my degree. I'd also discovered tennis after moving in at Alta Loma and became obsessed with playing, practicing about 6 hours each day. I got so good that I was able to play in tournaments. One doubles tournament I participated in was at producer Norman Lear's house, with another held at the Playboy mansion.

My Father's 'bar time' wasn't entirely without merit. He'd established one particular restaurant as his 'go-to' place and spent most of his downtime there. The SARATOGA was located near the corner of Fairfax Ave. and Sunset Blvd. It was a classic old Hollywood style restaurant with a big bar and lots of 'intimate' booths that provided the type of privacy celebrities would often seek. My father was now working for a company that provided security for many of the High-rise buildings in Los Angeles, and his position afforded him quite a bit of freedom. Almost every day, he could be found planted at the Saratoga's bar from about 4:00 pm onward. Gus, as he was referred to, had a way of charming people. He made friends easily and often would have drinks with the likes of director Hal Needham ("SMOKEY AND THE BANDIT" "HOOPER") or actor Chaz Palminteri ("THE USUAL

SUSPECTS"). His association with Hal lead him to become the Captain of the "Stunts Unlimited" softball team, which was part of a League of industry teams that played against each other at various local fields. I even got involved at one point and played some games with them from time to time.

One valuable association my father made at the Saratoga was with a man named Garrison True. Gary, as we called him, was an actor and occasional casting director. My father introduced me to him, and once I'd found out that Gary had been a 'red shirt' on Star Trek TOS, our relationship was a certainty since I was a huge Star Trek fan. Gary had done many episodic TV shows during the '60s and '70s and knew his way around Hollywood. He became something of a mentor to me and always had his eye out for projects I might be right for.

Side Note: From 1975 to 1976, I got involved with two workshops to better hone my skills in comedy and improvisation. In both cases, I was the youngest member that either class had ever allowed in. 'Harvey Lembeck's Comedy Workshop' was the more prestigious of the two, with such luminaries as Robin Williams, Penny Marshall, John Ritter, and Kim Cattrall having once been participating students. The 2nd one was with Tony Geary (General Hospital) & Jack Warfield (Hard Target). Just before I left to do a TV Movie on location, we put on a production called "Hollywood Next Seven Exits" at the Chamber Theatre on Cahuenga Blvd. It was a series of sketches that poked fun at everything Hollywood including the famous Universal Studios Tour, where I was the tour bus driver entertaining my passengers with movie trivia. Everything was improvised, so the audience got a different show each night!

As much as I loved Star Trek, I was also a diehard fan of "THE SIX MILLION DOLLAR MAN," which began airing on ABC in 1973. For its fourth season, the 7th episode was titled: "The Bionic Boy." When I got the call from my agent's office that I would be auditioning, I went nuts over the possibility of becoming a new Bionic character opposite Lee Majors!

For me, this was going to be the most important audition I would ever have, and desperately wanted to make sure I landed it. My mother had warned me not to get my hopes up, and in the end, she was right. It was common practice in the business to pre-cast a project but still hold auditions to give the Agents and the actors the impression that favoritism wasn't in play. It was also common knowledge that ultimately, the Networks had final say if they felt someone had better audience recognition. Such was the case with "The Bionic Boy." I'd come close, but the executives in charge at ABC weren't as familiar with me as they were with Vincent Van Patten, so Vinnie ended up with the role, and I was left devastated. Even today, I can't help but think how the trajectory of my career would have altered if I'd been given the part instead of Vincent.

A few very depressing weeks passed before I received an urgent phone call from Garrison. Gary had been visiting a casting director friend of his at the Universal casting offices when he called and asked me if I could rush on over to the studio for a last-minute audition. I said "yes" and jumped into my 1969 MGB-GT (my 1st car) and hauled ass over the Hollywood hills to Universal City. I made it in record time, parked, and ran into the casting offices where Gary was waiting. He hustled me into a room where a casting director named Geri Windsor was sitting with headshots scattered all over her desk. Geri was casting for a 2-part TV movie that Jack Laird was producing starring Bette Davis. "THE DARK SECRET OF HARVEST HOME" was based on Tom Tryon's novel 'Harvest Home' and would become one of the most expensive TV movies ever made.

"THE DARK SECRET OF HARVEST HOME"

"Here, read this," Geri said. She had her hand outstretched with a script in it and never looked up. I took the 'sides' (industry-speak for scene pages from the script), and Gary and I stepped out of the office to go over the material. About two minutes later, Geri came out and ushered me back in. She hadn't even given us time to review the material before having me read it with here. I gave it my best shot, and then she asked me to come to the parking garage with her. I thought it an odd request, but she said, "OK, let me see you move." "Move?" I asked. "Yeah, do a cartwheel or something.... Just show me you have good physicality." I took a few steps, then decided to use some of my saber choreography from my time spent in classical stage weapons training. I struck a pose and started dueling with an unseen opponent, jumping and swinging with an invisible sword. I leaped up onto the stairs, took a few more swings, then jumped off the 4th step onto the garage floor, with a resounding "Eh La!" "OK, that'll do." She said, "Come back in the office."

It was 5:00 pm, and Gary was still there waiting. She sat back down at her desk and proceeded to tell me the deal. "You'll be on location for about three weeks, and the salary is $1,800.00 per week plus $60.00 cash a day (per diem) for food. Flights, Hotels, and any other transportation we handle. Take it or leave it." I looked at Gary, who just nodded, and I turned back to Geri. "When does this start?" I asked. "You leave for Ohio in the morning at 8:00 am." I turned back to Gary. He nodded again without saying a word. My Agent always handled my 'Deal' negotiations, and I'd always just go along with whatever arrangements they cut, so this was a first. "Well, OK," I said. "Great, here's your plane ticket," she said, and handed me both a script and the ticket. "A driver will pick you up at 6:00 am to take you to the airport, and there'll be transportation for you in Ohio to take you to the Hotel in Mentor." I thanked her, then left the office with Gary following behind me.

Once outside, I turned to him and said, "What the hell was that?". He didn't speak; he just gave me a mischievous smile and said, "Have fun."

The date was September 2nd, 1977. The next day was my birthday. I would be traveling alone to Mentor, Ohio, and celebrating my 19th Birthday in an unknown Hotel. Yeah, sounds like fun.

The main reason that 'HARVEST HOME' was so expensive to make was Producer Jack Laird's insistence that it be shot entirely on location. No backlot, No sound stages. It was an unheard-of approach that was sure to bite the hand that that fed it. The locations called for large fields of corn in Connecticut, as described in the book, but Connecticut currently had no corn. The state of Ohio would have to substitute for Connecticut because it did have corn. During the three weeks that I was scheduled to be there, we'd be shooting in at least four local communities. Each community would provide the needed settings to create the town known as Cornwall Coombe, a small Connecticut village. Like Tryon's previous novel "THE OTHER," "HARVEST HOME was a dark tale rife with pagan ritualism. A factor that would play out in one of the remote 'Amish' communities where we filmed.

I checked into the Hotel that operated as the productions 'central command center' and then took my luggage to my room. The Hotel was a typical bland, non-descript mid-west accommodation that looked like any number of Hotels I'd stayed at over the years while on tour. It was about 3:00 pm, and I was hungry, so I walked across the street to Wendy's for a burger. Wendy's hadn't yet expanded west of the Mississippi River, so this was a real 'birthday' treat. I'd discovered Wendy's while touring in "MAME" and always made a point of going when there was one nearby.

I placed my order and sat down just as a few members of the crew came in. They spotted me and knew right away I wasn't a local. They came over and introduced themselves, asking what role I would be playing. My character's name was 'Jimmy Minerva,' a young farmer competing against 'Worthey Pettinger' played by Michael O'Keefe ("CADDY SHACK") for the honor of becoming 'Harvest Lord.' The large cast also included David Ackroyd, Joanna Miles, Rosanna Arquette, René Auberjonois, Stephen Joyce, Linda Marsh, Tracey Gold, and Norman Lloyd, just to name a few. I won't try to explain the plot here, as it would take too long. I suggest looking it up on IMDB or Wikipedia, and the show itself can be seen on YouTube if you're interested in killing about 3 hours.

The crew folk joined me at my table to get acquainted, and I happened to mention that it was my Birthday. A cheer went up, and one of them said we needed to celebrate, so he went to the counter and ordered a round of Frosty's for everyone. The gesture was a welcome sign that this shoot might not be so bad after all. We all finished our treat and headed back to the Hotel. Filming had been underway there for several days, which confirmed my suspicion that whoever had initially been cast in my role had either been fired or dropped out. It was the only logical explanation as to the last-minute audition the day before.

Based on the dollar figures that Geri had quoted, I was going to make about $6,600.00 for three weeks' work, less my agent's fee, even though they'd had nothing to do with it. As it turned out, my final tally was more than $14,000.00 due to inclement weather that turned the 3-week gig into a 6-week ordeal of boredom. The constant rain kept us from doing any outdoor filming, so once all the interior scenes were filmed, all we could do was hole up in our Hotel and wait. It was during one particularly complicated indoor sequence that I finally made my acquaintance with the legendary Bette Davis, and boy, was it a doozy.

It was a large crowd scene that took place inside a 'Town Hall.' The shot required multiple cameras to take in all the action, as there was a lot of business to capture. I'd have to hit several key marks to complete all my blocking. The scene established my ascension to 'young Lord' status as the entire community participated in a ritual that involved a large pile of corn that sat in the middle of the hall. When the signal was given, a group of people (myself included) would descend on the corn in the hope of being the first to discover "the neck." A specific ear of corn that has some essential significance to the selection of the next 'Harvest Lord.' My blocking required me to dig through the corn and ultimately find the 'neck.' The crowd would cheer as I stood up and turned towards a group of people who would then part and reveal 'The Widow' standing behind them. I would slowly walk towards the 'Widow,' hand her the ear of corn, which she snapped in half. She then hands it back to me and turns me towards the townspeople who cheer in delight at the newly crowned 'Young Harvest Lord. Final editing made all this happen much faster, but the timing while filming made it feel more complicated than it was.

During the blocking rehearsal for cameras, the 'Widow's' part was covered by Bette Davis' stand-in. I had been so focused on all my 'business' that I didn't recall hearing the Director say that the next go would be an actual take. We all took our respective positions, and the Director yelled, "Action." I dove into the corn, found the neck, stood up, and turned. The crowd parted, and there I was staring straight into the face of a screen legend. As focus had become my mantra since the 'Mame' incident in Las Vegas, I just kept going and finished the take. The Director yelled, "cut," and I stood there for a long moment, trying to process what'd just happened. A couple of seconds later, the 1st AD approached me and said that Ms. Davis would like to see me. I figured I was toast. The ominous tone he'd used to relay her request only heightened my sense of panic, making me sure I was about to be fired.

The AD gestured towards the back of the room, where 3 to 4 rows of old wooden folding chairs were lined up. Bette was sitting alone in the middle of the last row and glanced at me as I made way over. Right then, an image popped into my head of me walking towards the gallows where the hangman stood looking like a small old woman dressed in Black by the name of Bette Davis.

I shimmied my way between the rows to the chair next to hers and sat down. A moment passed before she turned to me. "I'm Bette." She said. "We didn't have the opportunity to meet before the take, so I wanted to introduce myself." I was stunned. Here was a ten-time nominated and 2-time Academy Award recipient, making a point to introduce herself to me! We chatted for a few minutes, and not only was I NOT going to be canned, but she'd complimented me on my professionalism when faced with the surprise of seeing her for the 1st time during the shot. My respect for her went off the charts. I'd heard that she was difficult and demanding to work with, which she was, but this personal moment we'd just shared overrode any 'diva' behavior I might have witnessed while on location.

"THE DARK SECRET OF HARVEST HOME" 1977

After the first two weeks of filming, the production moved from Mentor to Conneaut, OH. Our Hotel there was even more depressing than the first one, as it was located right off an Interstate with nothing around it except a small gas station/diner with a few pinball machines for entertainment. With all the downtime we had because of the weather restrictions, we spent many idle hours playing pinball or hanging out in each other's Hotel room. One whole floor had been reserved for the main cast, and we quickly turned it into a dorm room environment. Everybody left the door to their room open, and we would just hang out in whoever's room had the most action going on. Michael O'Keefe had brought his guitar with him, and someone else had brought some marijuana, so group singing and getting high was a regular occurrence. In all my years of being exposed to drugs and alcohol, I'd never once been interested in trying any of it. I'd seen firsthand what effect it had on my father, and as a focused performer, I didn't like the idea of being out of control. So, I saw no reason to start partaking now just because everyone else was. Now mind you, I never passed judgment and could care less what anybody did to enjoy themselves. I just know, for me, it wasn't something that I personally ever felt the need to do.

It rained steadily for two weeks before the sky cleared enough for outdoor filming to commence again. The exterior shots were the main focus now, and one of the communities we filmed in was still trapped in the past. The roads were dirt and only wide enough to provide passage for horse and buggy, and the buildings were hand built of wood and looked old and used. There was a large park area in the center of the town that provided the community a place to picnic and enjoy other outdoor activities. There was also a 'Town Hall' off the main street. The whole setting was like something out of the Twilight Zone - a town frozen in time. It was quaint, but something about it just felt 'off.' The feeling would intensify over the days ahead as Hollywood, with all its hardware and creative energy, would descend upon it, making the nearby Amish community very uncomfortable.

With the need for 'bodies' to fill the town and to act as locals for the various events taking place during a 'Festival' sequence, many men, women, and children were enlisted from neighboring areas. Much to my delight, some of the lovely young ladies around my age had become enamored with me, as they weren't used to having Hollywood celebrities in their midst. They could often be found hanging out with us when we weren't shooting, which I didn't mind one bit. Sure, I had a girlfriend back in LA, but I didn't see anything wrong with a few harmless flirtations.

Me & my horses, 1977

It was during the 'festival' scenes that I finally realized why the casting director wanted to see my physical capabilities. There were two 'contests' that the young Harvest Lords had to compete in. The first was a race between hay carrying flatbed sleds pulled by Percheron horses.

These horses, like Clydesdales, were enormous, so the stunt coordinator needed me to spend some training time mastering my sled with the horse attached. Luckily for me, the horse was gentle and cooperative, making the stunt reasonably easy. Simple at least during the trial run before they introduced Worthey Pettinger's huge tractor. The 'bit' consisted of a race between horses with flatbeds, but Worthy (Michael O'Keefe) uses a tractor instead. Just as the horse race nears the finish line, Worthey speeds past on his tractor to cross the finish line first. It's a blasphemous attempt to show the town's folk how much easier their work would be if they would only embrace more modern methods. Worthey is scorned by the bystanders and told, "It's against the ways." Well, the tractor's loud engine noise proved troublesome for me as it spooked my horse and made it difficult to handle. To drive the rig, you have to hold the horse's reigns while standing upon an aluminum flatbed, which is at ground level. It took everything I had to keep my steed under control and moving forward as the tractor barreled past - it's engine temporarily frightening the horse.

The 2nd physical challenge I faced was a pole shinny contest. 12-foot-high log poles had been hammered into the ground and then greased. It was our task to be the 1st to reach the top. There were three of us competing, Myself, Michael O'Keefe, and a stunt man that doubled for the 3rd contestant. I never really was good at this sort of thing, and the grease made it even more difficult. After struggling to get about halfway up the pole, I lost my grip and slid back down. Michael's post was left ungreased because he's supposed to win, so my downslide would work perfectly for the editor later during post-production.

You spend a lot of time waiting around while on set due to the time required for lighting and camera positioning, so conversations naturally crop up to kill that time. Two of my favorite people to talk with were Rene Auberjonois and Norman Lloyd. Rene was a Tony winner with an extensive Theatre background, and Norman had been a friend and associate of John Houseman's and had worked with Orson Welles and Alfred Hitchcock.

I could sit for hours and listen to Norman tell tales of working in Vaudeville, radio, theatre, and as a director. Today, at 105-years -old, he is the oldest living performer from those bygone days.

After a few days into filming at the 'Twilight zone' set, there was an incident. Bette had a private trailer where she could rest and go over her script. Luckily, she wasn't there at the time, but somebody chose to make their protest about our presence known by putting some bullet holes in her trailer! From that point on, the production increased security measures and made sure that Bette was always escorted wherever she went. The natives were restless over the type of material being filmed in their backyard, and cults don't get along with other cults, so to speak.

One night while waiting on set, I went over to watch Bette shoot a critical monologue. She stood stoic in front of a huge bonfire that lit her from behind as if she were a demon summoned from hell. The camera simply held on her as she delivered the speech and then very slowly dollied close to her to emphasize the moment. As I watched, I kept waiting for some sign of greatness in her performance, but I never saw it. The delivery, to me, seemed rather pedestrian and lifeless considering the impact of the speech. When it was over, I walked back to my trailer, thinking I'd either missed something, or she just wasn't as remarkable as she once was.

Several days later, I had the chance to see some of the dailies that had been shot that night. The production had rented a small theater in town to screen the footage, and a few of us actors were allowed to sit in with the director and the DP to watch. Bette's nighttime bonfire scene came up, and I sat there stunned. Everything I didn't see was up there on the screen. It was riveting. The subtleness of her delivery suddenly came alive, and I realized just how 'in command' of both the camera and the environment she was. She was glorious to behold, and every bit the actress she'd always been. I'd grown up in Theatre, where a broader approach was needed to reach 'the back of the house.' Instinctively I knew that the camera captured more detail, was more intimate, and required a more subtle delivery. But what I came away with that night after watching the footage was that 'less is more' when it came to film and to never underestimate the power of the 'lens.' Bette had done just that providing me with a master class lesson in screen performance.

The weather held, and I was able to complete all my scenes before heading back to LA. On the last day of filming, the production threw a party for the cast and crew back at the Hotel in Mentor. Bette was there and looking every bit the Hollywood Star in her elegant white dress and heels. She was 69 at that time but looked older. She was a small woman that stood all of five feet two inches tall. But her very presence filled the room. I'll never forget the sound of her laugh.

The final cost to produce 'Harvest Home' came in at around 12 million dollars. The foul weather conditions that had plagued the production in Ohio and held up production, eventually necessitated filming back at the studio in LA. About a weeks' worth of pickup shots were required to finish certain scenes that hadn't been completed or had problems due to the local logistics. None of my stuff needed to be reshot, so I went on my merry way after returning. "HARVEST HOME" aired on NBC on January 23rd & 24th, 1978 to mixed reviews, but nearly all were favorable to Bette as the rock that held it all together. Garrison thought this might be the perfect time to champion me at Universal and have them sign me on as one of their contract players. Some studios had a stable of actors that they could pull from for various supporting roles in both television and film. They would put you under contract with a guaranteed salary, whether you worked or not. The caveat was that you couldn't work for anybody else. I was in favor of it, but it never came to fruition, and the studio wound up discontinuing the contract player format a year or two later.

A GRADUAL DECLINE

Just before I turned twenty in 1978, I landed a small part in another ABC Afterschool Special called "The Rag Tag Champs." Like "ROOKIE," it was a baseball story, and this time I played an umpire. We shot most of it on one of the fields that I'd often played softball on with the 'Stunts Unlimited' team. I had little to no dialog, but work was work, so I took it. I'd still been living with my parents all this time and was ready to go solo. At the end of the year, I moved out into a place of my own. Even though I was no longer on the "THE ELECTRIC COMPANY," I was still earning good money from the residuals that came in yearly. The show was airing twice daily and had branched out to include foreign countries as well. Twice a year, I would go to the mailbox and find a check from CTW that was either for international airings or domestic ones. The amounts varied from 6-10 thousand dollars each time and helped create a portfolio that was rapidly growing. And there was also the trust money that my parents had kept aside.

Keep in mind that TEC was a PBS show and not a Network one. Had it been a Network show, the residual amounts would have been 2-3 times more then what I was receiving. That's why everybody wanted to land a Network show that would last at least three years. It would ensure syndication and keep money flowing in for years long after the show ended. I did okay, but not nearly as well as the "BRADY BUNCH" kids or all the young actors from say, "LITTLE HOUSE ON THE PRARIE."

Side Note: The COOGAN LAW, as it was known, was a child labor law that was passed in 1939 by the State of California in response to the plight of Jackie Coogan, who earned millions of dollars as a successful child actor only to discover, upon reaching adulthood, that his mother and stepfather had spent almost all of his money. This law was not in effect in NY, but as I mentioned, my parents were maintaining a trust fund for me with some of my earnings. At one point during the run of TEC, I was making about $45,000. A year which was huge back then.

I'd been in a rebellious state that started around my 16th birthday. After working steadily for eight years, I wanted a break, which led to some 'attitude' that started to show whenever I had to go on an audition. Trouble began when the casting directors took notice of it. Both my Agent and my Manager were getting negative feedback from the CD's who told them, "He's very good, but he has a chip on his shoulder." Well, nobody likes a 'problem kid,' so I started booking fewer jobs as the months wore on. By 1979 I wasn't working at all and had moved into a two-bedroom apartment with my friend Terry Lamfers. But a new issue appeared when it became clear that I was an obsessive-compulsive regarding cleanliness and order. Terry was the exact opposite, so "The Odd Couple" was alive and well and living on Laurel Canyon Blvd. in Studio City.

Garrison True, my mentor, was now working as a dialog coach on a TV show called 'SALVAGE 1" that starred Andy Griffith. Gary invited me over to the set on the Warner lot, and I finally got to meet Andy in person. Let me just say that Andy Griffith is everything you would expect him to be. The man you saw on Mayberry was precisely how the man was in real life. Andy was warm, charming, funny, and a great storyteller. During one of the breaks, he mentioned a book he had been in search of for a long time. I had a friend who worked part-time in a bookstore and had him track down a copy of what Andy had been looking for. When I came back to the set a few days later, I presented the book to Andy, who was thrilled to receive it. From that point on, Andy insisted I become a regular fixture on the set. I relished the wonderful stories he'd share, and yes, I did mention the comparison to him and Ron Howard I'd received for my performance in "ON BORROWED TIME" years before.

My mother had never really liked living in LA. She missed her family, and she missed teaching her kids from the Newington Children's Theater. I was about to turn 21, and since I was no longer living at home, she decided that there was nothing to keep her there. My father agreed that I was old enough to manage my career independently, and he packed up the two of them, and they moved back to Newington. For the first time in my life, I was entirely on my own and totally in charge.

Terry and I'd begun writing a screenplay together, and I also had a gorgeous blonde girlfriend to spend time with. Oh, I forgot to mention that I was now driving a killer red and black 1969 Camaro RS with a 327 under its hood. I was twenty-one and a full-fledged adult but still sported a face that made me look seventeen at best. It worked to my favor as an actor since I could play young (under 18), and the production wouldn't have to provide a teacher on set. However, in the real world, I still looked like a 'kid' to anyone else I interacted with. The frustration of 'not being taken seriously' was a constant source of irritation. Having worked as a professional for the last 13 years, I'd gained experience and knowledge beyond my years. My training and self-assuredness gave me the poise to present myself as an adult, but my youthful face betrayed the confident young man beneath. It was a curse that would plague me for years to come.

One perfect example of this came about just before my parents left LA to return home to Connecticut. I was riding a motorcycle that I'd purchased to tool around town on, and one afternoon, Hal Needham happened to see me pull into the Saratoga parking lot. Hal new I was an actor and approached me, telling me he was working on a new movie call "MEGA FORCE." Producer Al Ruddy was looking for actors who could ride motorcycles used by a secret army of international soldiers, equipped with advanced weapons and vehicles. I loved the idea, and Hal arranged an audition with Mr. Ruddy. It took all of 2 minutes for Al to tell me I looked too young to be an international soldier of fortune. I got a "Thanks for coming in." and quickly left the office. Hal's good intentions were just no match for the babyface on a big wheel.

Terry and I were still working on our first screenplay together entitled "SUBJECT: ERIC" it was an action/adventure story about a young "James Bond' like character who tries to find out about his 'blanked out' past. The 'missing childhood' metaphor was a definite stab at my own life experience, with the adult 'trained killer' aspect a wish-fulfillment from my desire to be taken seriously. Nothing ever happened with the script, but that didn't deter us from continuing to write together. What we couldn't do was continue to live together. My OCD eventually drove him nuts, and we decided to find separate accommodations. As luck would have it, just across the street, there was a 'bungalow' style apartment complex that had two identical units available directly across from each other. The rent was reasonable, allowing us to remain close without invading each other's space. We could literally sit on the front steps of our separate bungalows and hold a conversation. It was the perfect solution to keep Terry from punching me in the face for not cleaning his room. Michael Blake was also in the mix, and the three of us spent a lot of time going to movies and shooting mini movies on Super 8 film. We did a whole series of "Six Million Dollar Man" shorts where I played Steve Austin, and Terry played Oscar Goldman. We shot on locations all over town from Griffith Park to Mid-Wilshire, taking advantage of Hollywood's many iconic locales to use as our sets.

I'd managed to land a part-time job as a fitness instructor at Holiday Spa in Hollywood and made enough to cover my expenses. I still had my portfolio funds that continued to grow because of the TEC residuals, so money wasn't an issue. I was on my 3rd car now - a silver 1979 Pontiac Trans Am with an orange screaming eagle on the hood. It was a bitchin ride that got lots of attention when we cruised on Van Nuys Blvd on cruise nights.

My parents had settled back into an apartment at my Grandparent's complex on Hartford Ave. in Newington. And my mother had heartily been welcomed back to the Children's Theatre, where she wasted no time motivating a whole new generation of eager kids. My career accomplishments over the years had made me a legend in the community, and my mother's involvement gave her significant credentials that all the students and parents respected. It was a nice shot in the arm for my mom, but my dad was having trouble re-adapting to the slower pace of life. I came back for a visit at one point and spoke to her class about working in Hollywood. I even screened some of my super-8 films for the group who got a big kick out of my 'bionic' running and feats of 'bionic' strength. It was during this trip that I made friends with one of my mother's students by the name of Tom Shea. Tom had 'it.' That needed element that Loretta Marshal had spoken of that could spark a career like mine. We became fast friends, and it was clear that Tom wanted to transition into bigger and better things than just local theatre. He was about four years younger than I was and looked like a young Cristopher Reeves. All the girls fawned over him, and I found a kindred spirit who was a near carbon copy of myself in terms of energy, talent, and a desire for fun. I even extended my stay just so Tom and I could spend more time hanging out, writing comedic songs, and impersonating our favorite Muppet characters. Tom was like the younger brother I never had.

Shortly after I returned to LA, my father decided to come back and see if he could score another sales position in the Security industry. He wasn't having any luck in Newington, so he took a small apartment in Hollywood and, in no time, landed a job with a prominent security firm. He spent a few months making sure that his position was a lock and then, somehow, managed to convince my mother to come back and join him. It meant that she'd have to give up everything she'd re-established in Newington and leave her family yet again to satisfy my Father's need to be somewhere more exciting. She struggled with the decision, but the thought of being close to me again tipped the scale, and she agreed. She packed up her stuff and once more came west. It would prove to be a colossal error in judgment.

The apartment my father secured was on Poinsettia Place near Sunset Blvd. just behind the Ralph's Supermarket. It was a small one-bedroom on the 3rd floor, and luckily my mother didn't bring too much with her. She quickly made the needed domestic adjustments to make it a home for the two of them. She was also optimistic that issues surrounding their marriage and my father's social alcoholism might be resolved. Three months after she'd given up her life and family back home, my father left her for another woman.

THE BEGINNING OF THE END

The woman's name was Harriet Hart. She was the building manager at the Westwood Medical Plaza on the corner of Wilshire and Westwood Blvd.' just down the Street from the UCLA Campus. They had met at a BOMA (Busines Office Managers Association) mixer and made a connection. She even ended up hiring his firm to supply the security for her building.

Harriet's demeanor was in direct contrast to my mother's. She was edgy and spoke her mind. She was a working woman in what was considered a man's business. Harriet worked hard, played hard, and had no problem with spending time at the bar with my father, smoking, and drinking well into the evening hours. He took only one suitcase with him and moved into her apartment in West Hollywood overnight, leaving my mother stranded and alone. He'd been involved with Harriet for months before coaxing my Mother back out to LA, and there was no doubt in my mind that leaving her had been his intention all along. When my career took precedent over maintaining a normal family environment, and we left to spend time away for my work, I'm sure he felt abandoned. He'd held the fort down while we were touring around the country, so what better way to make her feel what he'd felt all those years alone. It was a cruel way to make a point, but as they say, payback is a bitch, and he'd apparently harbored resentment towards her for years. He'd passed up his shot at becoming Chief of Police in Newington; he'd stayed faithful, had given up bonding with his son, and he'd gotten tired of trying to make up excuses to his friends to cover for all of it. My logical mind could understand some of his reasoning, but my emotional side hated him for being heartless and manipulative. My anger and disappointment over his hurting my mother this way effectively severed the last tendrils of our relationship. Or so I thought.

My mother was my rock. Over the years of performing, she had been my travel companion, my advisor, my agent, my sounding block, and, most of all, my best friend. There were no topics that were considered taboo.

Sex, politics, movies, books, art, gossip, relationship advice, and more were all on the table whenever I had questions. My father knew it, and it ate away at him. It simmered under the surface all the time. He felt that the constant female control I was under by her, my agent, and my manager was making me soft. There was even a point when he accused me of being gay because of my hair and certain types of clothing I wore. I reminded him of all the girlfriends I'd had, the 'Booby show' in Vegas, and all the Playboy magazines I'd perused over the years. I never saw color, I never cared what religion somebody was, and I never judged people by what their sexual preference was. Hell, even if I was gay, so what? It shouldn't matter, but he needed something to poke me with to get under my skin and make his point. He'd had no say in my upbringing and was mad at being robbed of participating in my life. It was an honest assessment, but not an intentional one. All three of us were victims of circumstance. We'd been swept up by all the attention, all the tempting rewards that came with my being in the public's eye and given special treatment. It had become a drug for the ego. I was too young to see it or even understand it, and the adults around me controlling my momentum were certainly not going to make me aware of it. You don't derail the gravy train.

I did my very best to console my mother, but the devastation over being ripped from her home, after having finally settled back in, was too much to bear. I spent as much time as I could with her, but between my job at the gym and the fact that I lived in the valley limited my availability. Once again, fate stepped in when a studio apartment became vacant, smack dab across the hall from her unit in Hollywood. I took it and moved in. It was walking distance from the gym, so I was able to spend more time with her. Time that I knew was vitally essential in keeping her from going over the edge.

It was now the summer of 1982, and my father was making a desperate plea to return and try again. Things with Harriet were not going well, and she wanted him to move out. I warned my mother not to believe him and that he didn't deserve a 2nd chance. Unfortunately, against better judgment, she consented, and he came back home, dragging his one suitcase behind him. At first, his intentions seemed genuine, but gradually he started staying out later and later each night drinking at the Saratoga. He'd begun seeing Harriet again, and one night he just didn't come home at all. Two days later, when he finally returned, I could hear him arguing with my mother from across the hall. She was crying profusely, barely able to get words out her mouth, and I realized it was finally time for me to intervene.

I crossed the hall and used my key to enter the apartment. My father held back tears as he tried to explain his situation, but I was having none of it. I was enraged. I told him to shut up and pack his bag; he was no longer welcome here. "Leave us alone!" I yelled. "Nobody is benefitting from any of this. Your inability to decide on what you want is destroying all of us." "I don't want you in the middle of all this." He said. "I already am in the middle!" I yelled. "Don't you get it? I've been in the middle of this for the past eighteen years! You keep using me as a wedge to drive between the two of you. You're pissed because we never had the relationship you wanted, and you blame her for letting it happen! It's all of our faults! We're all to blame, and it's time to stop taking it out on each other and move on with our lives."

We were all crying by now, but I refused to allow the tears to soften my resolve. "Get your bag and go back to Harriet. let us live in peace." There was a long silence before he turned and went to the bedroom to pack his bag. I moved over to my mother, who sat on the couch, silently weeping, and put my hand on her shoulder. I didn't say anything; I just stood there waiting for him to emerge with his things. When he came out, he looked at both of us as if wanting to say something, but I cut him off before he did. "GO," I said and pointed to the door. He wiped his eyes and left.

It took some time, but eventually, things settled down, and my father was smart enough not to make any contact with either of us. I was still working at Holiday Spa, but just after the first of 1983, I quit. It was also when, on the recommendation of both my agent and my manager, I decided to take a break from show business. This decision would prove to be a fatal mistake as the industry is well known for adhering to 'an out of sight, out of mind' mentality. If you're not constantly in the face of the casting directors, they will quickly forget you're out there, and this can prove to be the death knell for a career.

Half a block from the location of our apartments, there was a small, very charming little house that had just become available to rent. I thought that a change in scenery might just be the ticket to help us both heal from all the trauma we'd been experiencing over the past year. I went to look and met with the owner who just happened to live right next door. The home was just as charming on the inside as it was outside, and I agreed to rent it. I don't know why, but out of courtesy to my father, I called him to tell him we were moving. The conversation was very cordial and without any drama. He even surprised me by offering to cover half the rent each month. I wasn't working, so rather than dip into my portfolio to make ends meet, I accepted his offer.

AFI Western, 1983

Mom and I moved in and set up house. She'd landed a job a few months earlier, working as the secretary to the Dean at the Yeshiva University and the Simon Wiesenthal Center on Pico Blvd. We weren't Jewish, but my mother's knowledge of the culture and faith combined with her skills as a coordinator was enough to land her the position. It was a good thing. It helped keep her mind off what happened with my father, and it gave her purpose. Everyone liked her, and many of the boys from the University would make a point to stop by and chat. With the fall semester about to start, she approached the school about putting on a play. Since it was an 'all-boys' school, she suggested doing "TWELVE ANGRY MEN," and even though the University had never done anything like this in its history, she managed to convince them to say 'yes'!

The Yeshiva was able to secure a stage in one of the annexes from Beverly Hills High School for the performance, and rehearsals took place in the university's lunchroom after classes. My mother was beaming. She was in her element. I was so happy to see her finally enjoying something after all the pain she'd suffered. It was a challenge, though. None of the boys had any training and never acted before. I got involved and functioned as a 'coach' to help them with their performances, while my mother stayed focused on the blocking and production requirements. Only two performances were scheduled, and we packed the auditorium for both of them. The boys did a great job for novices, and their parents were ecstatic to see their son's doing something so 'out of the norm' for the University. The respect and adoration my mother received was overwhelming, and it gave her a new lease on life. Or so I thought.

MOM:

I'd noticed over the past year that my mother had been losing weight. She'd been a shapely woman up until my birth but struggled to shed pounds after the pregnancy. Not so now. And she was also slowing down. She'd turned 54 in August of that year, and I turned 25 a month later. We would often go to the movies together, and I found myself getting frustrated with her pace while walking from the parking lot to the Theater entrance. She was always about ten steps behind me even though I wasn't walking that fast. I didn't give it much thought at the time, but I should have. It turned out she was keeping a secret. During her time back in Newington, she'd gone to the Doctor and was diagnosed with type 2 Diabetes. It scared the crap out of her as she'd watched her Grandmother lose toes and experience a host of other ailments due to the disease. She refused to go through that, nor did she want to be on Insulin for the rest of her life. She also chose not to reveal her diagnosis to anyone and instead went along drinking Coca Cola and eating chocolates like she always had. Day after day, she exacerbated her condition by taking in too much sugar with no control over her spiking blood count. That November, she started to complain about a cyst that formed on her back at the base of her spine. She argued with me about seeing a doctor, but I forced her to go, and they diagnosed a *Pilonidal Cyst*. The Doctor treated the cyst and sent us home with medication and instructions on how to cleanse and apply the needed creams and antibiotics.

Mom was deathly afraid that I'd find out about the Diabetes when the Doctor got the results of her bloodwork back, and her fear was validated two days later when he called me to reveal the findings. I now had the added task of administering her a daily injection of insulin along with her other meds. So far, I'd been following the instructions on treating her to the letter, but she seemed to be getting worse rather than better. She stayed in bed all the time and seemed incapable of getting up. I made meals for her, but they went mostly uneaten. On the 4th day, I needed to go out to refill one of the prescriptions. I made her a sandwich and set it next to her bed with a glass of water. She was lying on her side, facing away from me. I told her I'd be back shortly and to please eat something while I was out. I could hear her breathing, so I assumed she was asleep and left to run the errand. When I returned, I went to check on her. She was still in the same position and had not touched the food or the water. I tapped her shoulder and gave her a light shake. "Mom, wake up," I said. "Time to wake up and eat something." There was no response. I started to panic as I slowly turned her towards me and discovered that her eyes were open, but she wasn't responding to either my touch or my voice. It was like she was there but not there. I checked her pulse, which was faint, and immediately called 911. Five minutes later, an ambulance arrived, and the medics went to work on her. She'd fallen into a Diabetic coma and was close to death. They tried to put an intravenous needle into her arm but kept having trouble and blowing the veins with each new attempt. I was a mess. There was nothing I could do except watch the madness that was unfolding before me like some surreal nightmare. This was my mother, my rock, the most important person in my life, and I couldn't help her.

The medics were finally able to stabilize her. They put her in the ambulance and rushed her to Hollywood Memorial Hospital on Vermont and Hollywood Blvd. while I followed in my car. I parked and ran into emergency where they continued treatment before admitting her and placing her in a room. She was OK, but the Doctor who came in told me that she might have suffered permanent brain damage due to the length of time she was in the coma. "This is my fault!" I thought. "If I'd only tried to wake her before going out, this never would have happened! My God, what have I done?!" I tried desperately to process everything, but I knew I needed to call her sister Ellen whose family had moved to Cerritos, CA, from Florida some years back. Having her sister close had also been a Godsend after my father left. She had immediate family close again, and the two would often have lunch together or just hang out. My three cousins (Ellen's kids) had also relocated, so I enjoyed getting to know them better after many years of being on the road performing.

Ellen made the 30-minute drive from Cerritos in record time, and the two of us consoled each other while sitting with Mom as she lay comatose in her hospital bed. I told Ellen that I hadn't yet called my father to inform him of what'd happened. It was his Saratoga time, and with no cell phone or text capability in existence yet, I knew I'd have to call him there. Not the best place to hear news like this, particularly since Harriet was likely with him.

I called from the phone in mom's room and asked the bartender if my father was there. It took him a moment to check before coming back and telling me that he was indeed there. I asked to speak with him and then waited for him to take the receiver. The din of voices and tinkling glasses were audible in the background, along with an occasional burst of someone's laughter. The seconds seemed like hours until I heard him on the other end. His "Hello?" had a distraction to it like someone who was in the middle of something and wasn't expecting a call. It was short, with a tinge of irritation that came from being interrupted.

"Dad, it's me, Steve," I said. "Moms in the Hospital, and it's not looking good." There was a very brief moment before he responded. "What, Joan is where, what?" came back at me, as he was having a hard time hearing me because of the activity at the bar. "I said," a bit louder this time, "Mom is in the Hospital! She's not doing well; we may lose her!" I glanced at Ellen, who had a disgusted look on her face. "Where are you? Which Hospital?" he asked. "We're at Hollywood Memorial on Vermont. Get here as fast as you can. And don't bring Harriet." I answered. We both hung up, and I looked at Ellen, who offered only one word of comment. "Asshole." She said.

Side Note: In 1982, I attended a Science-Fiction Convention at the Bonaventure Hotel in downtown LA. While there, I made the acquaintance of a man named Alex Rivera. Like me, Alex was an avid fan of all things sci-fi, anime, comic book, and toy-related. Along with Star Trek, Star Wars was now part of the mix, and I had been amassing a collection of fan-made props and costume pieces. Alex and I struck up a conversation where I learned he was an actor/model with master builder skills in constructing and detailing scale models. I mentioned my frequent trips to a Japanese toy store in Little Tokyo to feed my Giant Robot fixation, and he immediately knew which store it was. That clinched it. We soon became fast friends spending many a day hanging out, talking toys, movies, music, books, and other topics of shared interest. Alex was eight years older than I was, but the age difference had no effect on the bond of friendship we'd established. Like Tom Shea in Newington, Alex had become a brother. But Tom had remained 3 thousand miles away, and Alex was here. Terry and Mike were still my dearest friends, but Alex and I connected on another level. He was the older brother who could offer advice and a shoulder to lean on that was safe and unjudgmental. Up until his unexpected death in 2016, our bond never wavered. I regret that I never got the chance to say goodbye. His friendship and his impact on my life are a gift that I will always cherish. May the Force be with you, my brother, always.

My father eventually arrived at the Hospital, delayed because he'd had to drive Harriet home before heading over. Ellen gave him a rather chilly reception, which he ignored, and then, in perfect Police mode, started grilling me for information about what happened. I could tell he was upset, but he was doing an adequate job of masking his feelings. The Doctor returned and informed us that there was nothing else that could be done, and we would need to wait for her to come out of the coma before an assessment of her faculties could be made. The idea that a woman with her intelligence could have possibly suffered brain damage was, for me, a travesty beyond belief.

Gradually, the three of us made our way out of the room and into the hall. Ellen and I planned to be there again in the morning, but my father had work-related meetings that he couldn't avoid, so he would check in with me as soon as he could. Ellen could barely keep her disdain in check as my Father turned and left to return to Harriet. The whole thing was just wrong on every level. Mom didn't deserve this. She'd given up everything so I could excel at my craft and lead a life filled with experiences that most people could only dream about. The man that I'd become was her doing, and I owed her everything. I owed her MY life.

When she awoke from the coma several days later but didn't know who I was. She was lucid but talking crazy and asking questions about things that'd happened years ago. The doctor said she might snap out of it as more time passed, but the odds were extremely low. All they could do was treat her Diabetes as best they could to bring it under control, and even that was an uncertainty. Mom spent 6 months in and out of the hospital for treatment, with most of it IN. The one time I did get her home, she proved to be impossible to manage due to her loss of memory and the medications that were needed.

Her condition continued to deteriorate, and on the night of April 6th, 1984, Ellen and I stood vigil at her bedside in the Hospital. The Doctor indicated that it would only be a matter of time before she went. "It might be hours," he said, "or it might take a day or two." There was no telling. All we could do was wait. Ellen knew I was starting to crack and suggested I go home for a while. She'd stay and call me if there was any change. I didn't want to leave but agreed to get some rest and then come back later.

I was numb with emotions as I drove back to the house. When I got there, Terry was there waiting along with a friend from an acting class named Tanya. Tanya was something of an enigma. We rarely got together, but whenever we did, it was hard to keep our hands off each other. We'd never gone 'all the way,' and for as long as I'd known her, she'd been in a committed relationship. So, our occasional dalliances remained just that, dalliances. We both had strong feelings for each other, but she seemed reluctant to break from her steady and hook up with me. She was a good friend with a heart of gold that was always there for me. I just wished it'd become something more.

We all went inside and shared some snacks while I relayed to them the current status at the Hospital. We hadn't spent more than 30 mins at the house before the phone rang, and Ellen told me she was gone. My world had just come to a crashing end. Terry and Tanya didn't have to ask what'd happened; the plaintiff cry that burst from my soul told them everything. I ran out the front door, jumped into my car, and sped out of the driveway with tears streaming down my face. To this day, I still wonder how I managed to get to the Hospital without killing anybody or causing an accident. I could barely see out the window because I was crying so hard. I was still awash with grief as I ran up the hospital's stairs to the floor where mom's room was. I stood at the base of her bed, hoping against hope that she would open her eyes and be fine, but it wasn't to be. I was now crying so loud that it was disturbing other patients down the hall, so Ellen escorted me to an empty room where I could release my grief and slowly begin to deal with the loss.

The perplexing thing was that just days before she passed, she awoke with complete clarity of mind. She knew where she was, who we were, what was happening, and that Ellen and I had been there for her the whole time. For a brief moment, 'Joan' had returned to us. But It would be the last time I would ever get to speak with her.

I was inconsolable. The grief of the loss was so overwhelming that I was shaking as if having a spasm. My mother was gone; my rock was gone; my world was shattered. What would become of me now? I had no real job, no career, no girlfriend, and no future that I could see. My father was there, but, as far as I was concerned, he was a lost cause. He could never get beyond the drink to have any kind of meaningful relationship with me. That ship had already sailed years ago.

Memorial services would need to be arranged, and my father's involvement was a necessary evil if it were going to happen with any reverence. So together, we went to Forest Lawn in Glendale to purchase a plot and casket with which to lay her to rest. Forward-thinking on my father's part resulted in the purchase of two parcels if either he or I would need to use one on some future date. It was a sobering thought but a necessary one.

Always the planner and always thinking ahead, my mother had left specific instructions regarding her memorial service. The consummate Director, I thought. She'd also left me a letter that I was to open only in the event of her death. The content was something that only a mother could write to her son, and her words were both loving and inspirational. I read it a half dozen times before putting it down. Even in death, she'd reached out and touched my heart with her love and encouragement. I knew then that as long as she remained in my heart and my memories, she'd always be there to offer advice and support when I needed it most. My rock hadn't left me; she'd just found a new way to guide me through life.

The service wasn't exactly as she'd requested, but I did my best to hit all the key points. I gave the eulogy and made sure the music selections she wanted were met. I even arranged for a Scottish Bagpipe player to be present at the burial site to play 'Amazing Grace,' which was her most precious request. The most surprising thing about the Chapel service was the turnout of students from the Yeshiva who attended. Many of the boys decided to break with tradition and attend the funeral. So many chose to come that the Chapel couldn't hold them all. Many had to stand outside, straining to hear the words that were honoring her time on Earth. It was a touching testament to the impact and influence she'd been in their lives.

When it was all over, I told my father I needed some time alone to mourn the loss and figure out where my life was going. He said he understood and to call him if I needed anything or just wanted to talk. I know he meant well; he was just the last person I would ever reach out to if I needed a friend. There was way too much water under the bridge between us, and it'd take another two years before I could bring myself to reach out and ask for his help. During the stretch, I would make some poor decisions that would cost me nearly everything, including a relationship that was just too important to lose.

AFTER EFFECTS

It took over a month before I could bring myself to box up her clothes from the closet and donate them to Goodwill. There were other items that I gave to her sister Ellen and various friends that I knew would appreciate having something to remember her by. By the end of that month, I also decided to move to new quarters as the house was proving to be more than I needed and a constant reminder of her passing. I told my rather unsympathetic Landlord I'd be vacating and secured a one-bedroom apartment on Sweetzer and DeLongpre in West Hollywood. It was a nice building, well maintained, and the rent was reasonable. Paco and I moved in and set up house. Paco was my Yellow Nape Amazon Parrot. In 1981 I'd decided to indulge my desire to get an exotic bird. I'd always been fascinated by parrots and thought it might be fun to have one. My research led me to a woman who lived in the Valley and raised a variety of Exotics. Every room in her house was home to a host of parrots from Macaws to Amazons and Cockatoos. As this was 1981, the 'Exotic bird importation law' was eleven years away from being passed. That meant that exotics were still being poached and shipped to the States without oversight. The law effectively made it illegal to continue this practice and to protect the birds from cruel methods of capture and transport.

As I made my way from room to room investigating the menagerie of avian choices, my eye caught a glimpse of something in her kitchen. There was a cage sitting on top of a table. The enclosure had two sections with one bird in each section. The bird on the left was a young African Grey, and the bird on the right was a very young Yellow nape Amazon; the nape referring to the back of the neck where a patch of bright yellow feathers grew. The youngling had no tail feathers and looked like a plucked turkey with a naked butt. The woman told me that the two had been in the same cage together, but the Grey had plucked the Napes feathers out. The Nape was only six months old, and the Grey was about a year, so it wasn't uncommon for an older bird to behave this way as part of establishing a pecking order. She'd separated them so that the Nape would stop being bullied and grow its tail feathers back. Exotics can be expensive, and if I was going to spend upwards of $800.00, I wanted to get a beautiful, fully feathered bird. FYI…$800.00 in 1982 adjusted for inflation comes out to just under $2,200.00 by today's standards.

I was feeling sorry for this little guy. By no means did he fit the image of what I'd wanted, but something about him was tugging at my heartstrings. The woman could sense my dilemma and suggested she take him out and let me interact with him to see what would happen. She had me sit at her dining room table and brought 'Paco' out. At six months, he was only about half of what his eventual full-grown size would be. She placed him on the table where stood for a minute trying to figure out where he was. He kept looking at me, cocking his head from side to get a better view. My right arm was resting on the tabletop, and he decided that it looked like something he wanted to check out, so he made his way over and stepped up onto my wrist. I kept still so as not to spook him, and then very slowly, he began to make his way up my arm to my shoulder by the right side of my head. A Parrot's beak is a formidable weapon, so I remained motionless to keep him from possibly striking. He continued to look at me as if assessing me just like I was doing with him. A few seconds later, he stepped closer and tucked his head into mine, rubbing his cheek up and down on my neck. The woman smiled and said, "I think he's made his decision." I was instantly smitten. This little bird had made my choice for me! He'd picked me before I even had a chance to assess if he was the right one or not. I told the lady that I needed to get the necessary cage and supplies before I could bring him home and would return shortly to pick him up. She agreed, and off I went to go shopping.

Now, 40 years later, Paco is still with me and going strong. The bond between the two of us is almost symbiotic. Parrots are highly intelligent and also very affectionate. In the wild, they mate for life and are often known to die of a broken heart if their mate is killed. Their intelligence, however, can also prove to be an immense pain in the ass. He knows just how to push my buttons and is jealous of anyone who gets too close to me. After 23 years of marriage, my wife still can't get near me if he's on my shoulder. He'd just as soon bite her face off than let her in my space. Oh, did I mention that my wife is a Saint and very understanding? Not very many people would put up with his behavior and occasional screaming fits. It's typical Parrot comportment and can prove to be quite the challenge for a marriage. That's why we have dogs to even the playing field.

Paco and I settled into our new apartment, and I was spending time with Alex and generally treating myself to whatever I wanted. I had zero income but had money in the bank from the residuals. The underlying psychosis at this point, which I wasn't aware of, was that spending money and buying stuff made me feel better. And since there was no one around to keep me in check, it wasn't long before I'd used up my savings and found myself in significant financial trouble. I'd stayed in constant touch with my Aunt Helen after Mom's death, but she had no clue about my spending excess. Instead of turning to drugs or alcohol like so many others in the business, I used shopping to ease my pain. Like drugs, the fix was only temporary, which of course, would necessitate even more spending to keep the demons at bay.

Helen was working for Texaco Corporate in a high-rise near Downtown LA. I called her to have lunch, as my situation had passed the point where I couldn't cover my rent or the payment on my leased car. It was time to bite the bullet and let Ellen know what had happened. At first, she was both mad and astonished that I'd blown everything I'd worked for, but quickly understood the dynamic that took place without my mother around to manage my behavior. Because mom had always been the one to oversee my life and the finances related to it, no one had ever taught me how to budget or manage money matters. I hadn't been taught the necessary skills to lead a life outside of show business. Money that came in from CTW was deposited and spent knowing that more would be on the way. It never occurred to me that the residual amounts would drastically decline and would stop altogether once the show ceased airing re-runs in October of 1985. Oh, that trust fund my parents had supposedly kept for me?...... amounted to almost nothing. Much more of it, then I realized, had been used over the years to cover the costs of multiple apartments on both coasts and the moving-related expenses required every time a relocation happened. Even the additional fees for Mom's funeral came out of this fund as my father didn't have any savings to speak of to contribute. I was effectively broke after years of being the primary breadwinner at an age when I shouldn't have even been working at all!

Ellen was there for me after mom passed, and she did her best to fill her shoes as a surrogate mother of sorts. But she had three young adults of her own to contend with, and I didn't want to burden her by adding my life's trials and tribulations to her big load. Instead, when she asked how things were, I always replied, "Just fine," never alluding to any money or emotional issues that she could have provided me with guidance or advice with.

At the end of lunch, Ellen wrote me a check to cover my expenses. She told me that she'd help as long as she could, but I needed to get a regular paying job to support myself and to put a cap on the continued spending. Since I had no 'disposable funds' left, the splurging had no choice but to come to an end. Rent was my primary and most critical expense, so I knew that I'd have to reduce it. I'd already dealt with the leased car and was now driving a new Suzuki Samurai that'd just hit the market in 1985. My father had helped with the down payment, and it's super low price kept my payments manageable.

Terry Lamfers had married, and he and his wife Nancy had bought a condo in Lake View Terrace just outside LA proper. Nancy had also just given birth to their first child, a girl named Jessie. I was honored to be asked and accepted the role of Godfather, but true to form, I made for a really lousy Godfather and must sincerely apologize to Jessie for my lack of 'awareness' when it came to birthdays and other Godfatherly like duties.

Lake View Terrace was about 30 minutes from where I was by freeway, and they had a spare bedroom. They offered to rent me the room for a modest amount to help me out as long as I looked for work and ultimately landed a job. I thanked them and agreed to the conditions. So, again with my father's help, I secured a storage unit to put all my 'stuff' in, taking only Paco and the bare necessities with me to Terry and Nancy's.

It was fun at first being part of a family and always having something going on. Terry was still working at Universal, and Nancy was a stay at home mom. Terry and I never stopped writing together during all the stuff that had transpired over the past six years. Our latest project was something that had been inspired by my passion for Giant Robots and my desire to see a 'Live-Action' version on the big screen. It hadn't been done yet, mainly due to the extensive special effects required to produce it. CGI was barely in its infancy and had only been used thus far on Disney's "TRON" and Universal's "THE LAST STARFIGHTER." It was faster and cheaper than practical effects but only worked best, from a visual standpoint, in computer looking environments like depicted in "TRON." Real-world objects and locations were far too complicated for the current state of computer capabilities to render believably. We had no intention of using CGI anyway as we wanted the film to have a tactile feel to it. We wanted the audience to believe our creations were real robots, something you could walk up to and touch, not computer renderings that looked artificial and out of 'touch.'

After four months of living with the Lamfers, I found myself not holding up to my end of the bargain. I hadn't looked for work and was now indebted to them for the rent that they had let me slide on since I'd moved in. Nancy's patience was wearing thin, so when Terry approached me about the past due rent, I knew I had pushed things too far. With a great deal of difficulty, Terry told me that if I couldn't come up with all the back rent by the end of the week, they'd have to ask me to leave. It was a sobering moment. It meant that my problems had now become their problem, and I'd put Terry in a position of having to do something so drastic that it would effectively end our relationship. I needed to immediately get my shit together and make good on my promise if I was going to salvage the situation. We both had tears in our eyes as he waited for me to respond. I could hardly blame him for the ultimatum. His family came first, and I'd proved to be both a dishonest friend and a liability. Sacrificing me was a necessary step to maintain his family's future.

"I'm sorry," I said. "I never meant to put you in this position. I know how difficult telling me this is for you. You and Nancy have every right to toss me out on my ear. I haven't kept my promise, and it's created a rift between you and your wife that never should have happened. I'm responsible, and it's up to me to fix it." I stood up and faced him, "You'll have the money by Friday, or I'll pack my bags and leave. If I do, I want you to know that I will always love you and your family. You're doing what's right, and I'm grateful to you for the time we've spent together all these years." I walked away, went to my room, and closed the door.

Now alone in my room, the tears began to flow freely. I was lost and alone again without the means to pay them by Friday. Paco and I were now on the brink of living in my car, homeless. Too much protection and one-sided experience in a business that only chose a select few to succeed had abandoned me without the skills needed to live and work in the 'real world.' Performing had been my life, and the success I'd achieved had convinced me that it would only continue throughout my adult years. I saw no need to prepare for something else. My career was a lock. I had the talent, and everybody loved and adored me. Why should my life take a different path then what had clearly been mandated by divine destiny? "How egotistical," I thought to myself.

Later that night, I picked up the phone and called my father to tell him what was about to happen if I didn't right the wrong that I had perpetrated on Terry and his wife. He said he'd cover the amount I owed them and knew of a possible job if I was interested. Desperate for anything, I asked him what it was. He said he'd gotten wind of a new security staff being assembled at Drexel Burnham Lambert located on Wilshire Blvd. in Beverly Hills.

He knew the recruiter who was doing the hiring and would recommend me if I was interested. I didn't care what it was. I wanted in and a chance to fix things. It was Monday. On Wednesday, I went in for the interview then swung by the Saratoga to pick up a check from my father. Thursday morning, I gave Terry and Nancy the back rent I owed them, and on Friday morning landed the security job. I'd somehow managed to come through and keep the promise I'd made. I still had no idea if I could handle the new position, but I was determined to make the best of it and approach it like I would any job. The assignment took on a life of its own once I got started.

DREXEL BURHAM LAMBERT:

It was now 1986, and I had started working as a Security Officer at a large Financial firm known as Drexel. It was the home of a High Yield Bond trader by the name of Michael Milken. The firm had hired Twelve of us to operate three shifts around the clock in the same building where world-famous 'Gumps' (a highly expensive gift store for the rich and famous) was located on the 1st floor. We were a uniformed team that looked exactly like an LA Sheriff, same colors, similar badge & patch placement, and duty belts but without the guns. At first, they allowed us to wear our uniforms to and from home, but after one too many incidents where we were mistaken for actual Sheriffs, a locker room was provided to suit up on-premises.

As the least experienced member of the team, I initially pulled the graveyard shift, which was from 11:00 pm to 7:00 am. However, it didn't last for long. I presented myself so well and provided such excellent nightly log reports that I was transferred to the day shift in no time. 7:00 am to 3:00 pm became my new hours, along with a small boost in pay. The salary was amazingly decent for 1986, and in no time at all, I was able to support myself and keep things current with Terry and Nancy.

Terry and I continued to work on our screenplay, which had the original title of "BATTLESUIT" but later changed the title to the acronym "B.R.U.T.E." (Battle Robotic Unit Test Edition) because we'd discovered that there was a tabletop game called "BATTLESUIT." To assist the reader with a visual reference, I designed a "Users Technical Manual' to present along with the screenplay. It provided detailed information about the Robot, its weapons, its power supply system, and all the other 'Tech' we'd created for the "B.R.U.T.E." universe. We even commissioned an artist to produce drawings for the designs.

We wanted to make a presentation that would stand out from the usual script offerings. To generate some 'buzz' about the project, we also took out a small teaser ad in VARIETY that had a silhouette image of the Robot along with an epic and mysterious description of what it was:

IT STANDS 70 FEET HIGH

IT WEIGHS OVER 40 TONS

IT'S THE MOST POWERFUL WEAPON EVER CREATED BY MAN....

AND IT HOLDS THE FATE OF THE WORLD IN THE PALM OF IT'S HAND.

The logline and designs worked, snagging us a Literary Agent who immediately began submitting the project around town.

After six months of working at Drexel, I'd saved enough money to finally rent a place of my own again. I didn't want to burden Terry and Nancy any more than I already had, plus the drive from Lake View Terrace to Beverly Hills and back every day was proving tedious. I quickly found an apartment in a brand-new building located in North Hollywood and moved in. I had all my stuff back, and my drive to work took half the time it did from Terry's condo. Things were definitely looking up.

Part of what we did during our shift was to patrol the building. Everything was key-card access, but there was always the chance that someone could find a way in or get somewhere they weren't supposed to be. The firm was generating enormous amounts of money from what the banking industry referred to as 'Junk Bond Trading,' putting Mr. Milken, and many other top traders, at risk of becoming targets. Corporate buyouts and Hostile takeovers could cost people their jobs, and Drexel was famous for them. It was big business, but the little guy who lost his income from the coup might want to vent his anger on the people responsible for his plight, IE: The traders.

One day while on patrol through the lower level garage area, I spotted something unusual. The garage was gate accessed from the street between the Drexel building and The Beverly Wilshire Hotel. At the bottom of the first level, there was an additional security gate that the traders and Mr. Milken's personal driver/bodyguard could open via key card. The access led to a private secured parking area at the base of the primary elevator bank. When you left, your vehicle would have to trigger the sensor that activated the gate. The procedure necessitated a full stop while you waited for the gate to open before moving forward. It occurred to me that this was a potentially vulnerable spot as the waiting time could allow someone to have access to the vehicle and potentially cause harm to its passengers. It was a gap in security that appeared to have gone unnoticed.

As I walked the area, I made a point of checking for places where someone might hide something (such as a weapon). I turned my gaze upward to the ceiling, lined with electrical conduits and pipes that lead to and from the various floors. This is where I spotted the knife. At first, I only saw the handle, but upon closer inspection from a different angle, I could see light reflecting off the large serrated blade. From its position, it had clearly been placed there with purpose.

I radioed my supervisor in the main office upstairs and asked him to come down to the garage. I didn't want to broadcast my findings to the whole team and create a stir that might find its way to Mr. Milken and the other traders. My immediate supervisor arrived, and I pointed up at the knife. He was tall and reached it easily, holding it carefully to not disturb any possible fingerprints. He looked it over, then looked at me and asked, "How the hell did you find this?" I told him my observation of the potential security gap and my subsequent investigation of any possible threats. He nodded then radioed for the department head to join him down in the garage. When he arrived, my supervisor showed him the knife and relayed to him how and why I'd discovered it. Two things happened shortly after this. One was a change to the garage gate entry/exit protocols, and the second was my promotion.

After spending a year in uniform, I was now given a stipend and told to purchase myself business suits, which would become my new attire. My official position was that of Team Supervisor acting as a go-between the uniformed staff and the department heads. During the day, my station was a security desk located on the 5th floor across from reception. This was the 'trading' floor. There were some individual offices and four conference rooms, three small and one large, with the trading floor itself taking up half the space on the Northside of the building. It was accessible through only two doors located on either end of a long hall, and you could only access the doors via keycard. My desk had monitors showing both entrances and a rear elevator on the opposite side of the hall. It was a private elevator used only by Senior staff and their personal assistants. I monitored the comings and goings of all personnel to the trading floor and would walk the trading floor several times a day to give the staff an added sense of security. Oh yeah, my salary also got bumped again.

I was now in a high-profile position due to my presence on the trading floor and my visibility in reception. From politicians, show business celebrities, and sports stars to international banking contingents and Foreign Dignitaries, anybody who was anybody had to pass my way. My experience working with these kinds of people during my career made me a natural for the job. My manner and my communication skills and understanding of these personality types made me a valuable asset that didn't go unnoticed.

Terry and I's Literary Agent continued to submit our project to various Studios and Production companies, but it wasn't getting much traction. Nobody could visualize how a project of this scope could be accomplished without costing a fortune. We knew how to do it, but without ever getting a meeting with anybody, we couldn't relay the concepts. We were obviously ahead of our time as years later; with the advent of sophisticated CGI, "Transformers' became a box office sensation. At one point, our Agent indicated that Telepictures was interested, but nothing ever came of it.

We also found ourselves 'too soon' on another genre front. The world of comic book superheroes had not yet been explored, and we couldn't understand why. There were many characters and stories just waiting to be exploited for the big screen, and no one was making any effort to tap into it. Terry and I decided to take a chance by creating a 'spec' script for the Marvel character "IRON FIST.' We drafted a spec screenplay based on the comic's first issue and the origin story of Danny Rand and his journey to becoming the 'IRON FIST.' We stayed true to the comic book authors' presentation making only minor changes for cinematic clarity and possible budget restraints. We commissioned another Artist to create a mock Movie Poster depicting the main character surrounded by a collage of scenes from the story. The artist was a young man whom I'd met during my time at Holiday Spa. He was a very talented but untapped illustrator who should've gone on to great things. For some reason, he never got the breaks and faded off into obscurity, yet another victim of people with a lack of vision.

I got wind of a Stan Lee appearance being held at a comic book shop in Studio City. When the day arrived, Terry and I grabbed our script and 'Poster' and went to see if we could get in front of Stan with our idea. There was a break in the crowd by the desk he was sitting at signing autographs, and we jumped in. I set the script down in front of him and held the framed poster up so he couldn't miss it. We didn't say anything; we just let him look and let the materials speak for themselves. He nodded and asked if we had an agent. I said yes, and he said, "Okay," I'll look at it and get back to you." We left him our number and walked out feeling like we had made a breakthrough. His interest could turn out to be our chance to get Hollywood to pay attention to a genre waiting to be unearthed.

A week later, we got a call from Stan's secretary. She said Stan liked what he saw and to call his agent. We called, and an appointment was set up for us to speak with him. I remember that he was very dismissive but willing to see what we could do. He asked us to put together two outlines, One for IRON MAN and the other for THOR. We spent a solid week of all-nighters to create the requested drafts, and I dropped them off at the man's office hopeful that we might get the assignment to write the screenplay for one, or maybe both of them. In typical Hollywood fashion, we never heard from him again. It would take another 20 years before Marvel Studios, and Paramount Pictures would produce the first blockbuster superhero movie based on "IRON MAN."

Things at Drexel were going exceptionally well. I'd made a good impression on the Senior staff and had also managed to make a good impression on one of the lovely personal assistants. Her name was Rachel Winter. I'd met and spoke with Rachel on many occasions regarding work-related topics, but we'd never spent time outside of work together. Since my mother's death, I hadn't pursued romantic relationships, but not for lack of trying. There were women whom I was attracted to; they just weren't attracted to me. Tanya and I had gotten together a few times over the past several years, but the end result of the evening was always the same. Things would go just so far before she would dismiss herself and head home. To this day, I can't figure out why she couldn't or wouldn't consummate the connection. Only she knows the answer, but for me, it will forever remain a mystery.

On occasion, my father would stop by Drexel whenever he was in the neighborhood for a sales meeting or check-in with an account. He was delighted to see that I'd excelled in the position and was moving up the ladder. My financial worries seemed to be behind me, and I was succeeding at something other than performing. I missed being in the limelight terribly but kept my focus on the present and where it might lead.

I don't recall the exact circumstances as to how Rachel and I hooked up. What I do remember was that a party was involved that ended with the two of us going back to her place.

Our relationship was complicated. Rachel was six years older than I was, my height, blonde but not a beauty in the traditional sense. She had something else. A softness that made her instantly approachable and a physical aura that was intoxicating. I found myself drawn to her anytime she was near.

Like any relationship, we began to find out more and more about each other's pasts as things progressed. We spent weekends together and the occasional weeknight, but I began to sense she was having concerns about us being a couple and working at the same place. We both knew people were talking, but it didn't bother me. It was the first real adult relationship I'd ever had with a woman, and I was in love, but there was a dynamic at work that I didn't realize until years later after I had the chance to analyze why it failed.

They say we often fall for people with some of the same traits and qualities as our parents. It's an unconscious attraction that provides us with a comfortable feeling of safety and familiarity. I was attracted to Rachel because of her softness, intelligence, and patience. Traits that were very much a part of my mother's makeup. However, the other side of her personality included both alcohol and drug abuse problems from years before I'd met her. Habits that would turn her temperament around on a dime when she partied too hard or got depressed and used drink or drugs to ease the hurt. She was a two-headed coin with my mother's face on one side and my father's face on the other. I'd managed to find both my parents rolled into one, effectively putting myself right back into familiar territory.

My desperate need for a 'feminine' connection that was lost when mom died drove my behavior to extremes when Rachel's erratic personality would cause her to 'disappear' for several days at a time to party freely without my involvement. I'd become so distraught over the idea that she would lose control and sleep with someone else, I'd drive over to her apartment and park just far enough away to wait and watch to see when she would come home, and if anyone was with her. The obsessive fear I felt over possibly losing her to someone else, and my constant need for reassurance eventually pushed her too far. When I proposed marriage in one last desperate attempt to secure her love, she declined because she knew it was driven by my fear of being alone and not from any real desire to marry. The relationship ended shortly after my 30th birthday. It was the first and only time that I'd considered suicide as my only option to end the pain.

I owned a 9mm that I bought from Alex when he was hard up for cash one time, which I kept in a case at the bottom of my closet where I could easily access it in an emergency. I was now living in a new studio apartment on Poinsettia Pl. between Franklin and Santa Monica Blvd. It wasn't the best neighborhood, but I liked the apartment and its proximity to Drexel's offices. I'd even struck up a friendship with another actor who lived downstairs from me by the name of Reginald Vel Johnson. Reg was still basking in the breakout fame he'd recently acquired playing Sgt. Al Powell opposite Bruce Willis in "DIE HARD." We'd share an occasional beer and talk show biz, but his career was accelerating, and his casting as the male lead in the ABC sitcom "FAMILY MATTERS" effectively ate up all his time, so I didn't see much of him after that.

Drexel was now in the thick of being investigated by the SEC over insider trading, stock parking, manipulation, and securities fraud. Mr. Milken had been identified as a key player and was forced to leave the company. I watched in anger as numerous traders I knew and worked with were taken from the trading floor in handcuffs because of Rudy Giuliani's witch hunt. Once the 'big guns' were rounded up, the rest of the remaining staff were also let go. They offered me the opportunity to stay for an additional three months, but I opted to leave and get on with my life. I also wanted to get away from the painful memories of the time I'd spent there with Rachel. It was the end of an era for Drexel, and the end of my relationship.

Christmas of 1989 was now upon us, and I was alone again. As the Holiday season often did, severe depression set in as I had no idea where my life was going at this point. I'd tried before to rekindle my acting career in 1985 but found myself confronted by a whole new regime of young Agents and Casting Directors, who didn't know me and didn't care what I'd done in the past. The industry had changed while I was away, and my membership had been revoked. I'd have to start from scratch if I wanted to get back in.

On one night, sometime between Thanksgiving and Christmas, I found myself in an exceptionally depressed mood. I couldn't stop thinking about everything that had happened to me and how much I'd lost. Tears were streaming down my face, and the despair I felt drove me to the closet and the cased 9mm. Maybe this is what it'd come too. Perhaps this was the solution to putting a stop to any more disappointments and feelings of abandonment. How many times could I pick myself up, brush myself off, and invest myself in something or someone that would ultimately reject or abandon me? One trigger pull would end all the misery, all the self-loathing that'd come from making too many bad decisions.

I pulled the 9mm from the case and chambered a round. I stared at the gun for a long time before raising the barrel to my mouth. At that moment, an image popped into my mind of the next day's headline reading: *'Former Child Star Commits Suicide Inside Hollywood Apartment, No One remembers who he was.'* In that instant, I started to laugh. "Oh, how dramatic," I thought to myself. "Once an actor, always an actor." I put the gun down, pulled out the magazine, and ejected the bullet. I put everything back in its case and then back into the closet. While wiping the tears from my eyes, I continued to laugh out loud at my self-aggrandizing Newspaper headline. Life, as I was about to find out, still had more to offer me.

Side Note: Shortly after I'd left Drexel, I took a receptionist job at a well-known Modeling Agency. My job was to assist in handling the front office and seeing to the needs of the agents. All-day, every day, prospective models would come in hoping to be the next 'big thing,' but 99.9% of those that did, didn't stand a chance. Many had spent hundreds, if not thousands of dollars on professional photos to create their portfolios, for the agents to consider.

I would take them back to the pit where the agents would proceed to chuckle, sneer, degrade, insult and dismiss the contents of the portfolio before telling me to tell them, "Don't quit your day job." I hated every minute of it. These people that came in had a dream, and I had no right to be the one to tell them that they had no chance. Instead, I would just offer an "I'm sorry, but you're not the type they're currently looking for." It was a brutal business, and I couldn't wait to get the hell out of there.

There was one good thing that came from working there, though. The agency had a commercial department that represented many of its clients for both print and television commercial work. Brad Pitt (who needs no introduction), Djimon Hounsou (AMISTAD, GLADIATOR), Joel Gretsch (THE LEGEND OF BAGGER VANCE, MINORITY REPORT), and Johnathon Schaech (THAT THING YOU DO) would all come in and just hang out with me in the reception area. None of them, including Pitt, had their big break yet! They would grab drinks from the refrigerator and plop down on one of the couches to 'shoot the shit' with me. They were all great guys who went on to establish careers they could all be proud of.

CAROL, THE COLONY & DISNEY:

I first met Sandy Tucker when we lived on Alta Loma Rd. Sandy was an aspiring actress who lived a couple of floors below us, who I'd often play tennis with. Sandy was like a sister to me, and we'd stayed in touch with each other after the move from Alta Loma Rd. to North Hayworth Ave and Sunset Blvd. in 76'. Sandy had once been a roommate of Majel Barret (Rodenberry) when Majel was first dating Gene Rodenberry and playing 'Nurse Chapel' on STAR TREK back in the 60s. Sandy always got invited to the Rodenberry's every Christmas, and one year, took my copy of the Star Trek Technical Manual with her for Gene to sign. Gene was known for imbibing a bit much and signed the book, 'Prosper and live long.... Gene Rodenberry'. The actual saying is (Live long and prosper), so my autographed copy has the unique distinction of having been influenced by Gene's slightly tipsy state of holiday cheer.

Sandy called me on Christmas eve day and asked if I'd go with her to a party held by some of her Theatre friends in North Hollywood. I declined at first, but she insisted it would be good for me to get out and stop feeling sorry for myself. "You need to shake it off and give yourself the chance to see what else is out there." She told me. "These are fun people, and you can talk Theatre to your heart's content. I'll come to pick you up around 7:00." I said, "OK" and hoped it wouldn't turn out to be a mistake that would end up making me feel worse than I already did.

We could see and hear the party spilling out onto the apartment's 2nd-floor balcony as we parked and walked across the street. We got to the front door of the apartment just as someone opened it to get some air. We said hello and then entered into a sea of people illuminated by lights from a sizeable Christmas tree in one corner of the living room. Holiday music was playing, and a group of people had gathered in the kitchen surrounding a table with all the usual holiday food offerings. We made our way towards the group where the host and hostess were standing in animated conversation with several guests. The hosts were Sandra Kinder and Don Woodruff, both of whom were resident members of the Colony Studio Theatre in Silverlake.

I scanned the food table just as Sandy made the introductions. There was an impromptu bar set up on a counter at the edge of the kitchen, where I poured myself some eggnog then glanced around the living room. When my gaze got to the Christmas tree, it stopped. Standing next to it was a vision. A 5-foot 2-inch vision of loveliness with shoulder-length reddish/blonde hair, and she was staring back at me. I smiled, then she smiled, so I made my way over to find out who she was. Her name was Carol Newell, and she, like most of the other guests in attendance, was a member of The Colony Theatre. I was surprised to find out that she was there alone and didn't appear to be involved with anyone. We had a great conversation going that she laced with an occasional flirtation that provided a much-needed boost to my recently shattered male ego. I started thinking that there might be hope for me after all, and Sandy had been right to insist on my coming along. I could hardly believe it when we exchanged phone numbers and made a plan to talk soon and have lunch together.

Sandy and I finally left and headed back to my apartment for the drop-off. On the way, she told me that she knew Carol through Don and Sandra and that Carol recently divorced from her actor/husband, Richard Lineback (SPEED, TWISTER, TIN CUP, THE JACKAL). Richard was still a member of the Company, but they'd parted amicably, and she was moving on with her life. Sandy was delighted that I'd made a connection and wanted to know all the juicy details once we'd had our lunch.

I called Carol the day after Christmas, and we made plans to meet at her place of work in Downtown LA after the Holiday break. A week later, I made my way downtown to a location in the warehouse district, where she had an office at a restaurant supply distribution company. We went to a place nearby that she knew and immediately picked up our conversation from the party the week before. She was delightful—a tiny package of effervescence that was both cute and sexy at the same time. The connection was swift, and the romance began in earnest. Oh, I forgot to mention, she was ten years older than I was.

Headshot, circa 1990

Three months later, I gave up my apartment in Hollywood and moved in with Carol. She had a one-bedroom on Rowena Ave. in Silverlake, but not big enough for all my stuff, so I'd need to rent a storage space nearby. We set up house together while I continued to work at the Modeling Agency.

Before I'd left Drexel, I'd started solo work on a new script. The action/horror genre had become very popular in the late 80s, so I figured it was a perfect time to jump on the bandwagon. In 1971 a film entitled "THE OMEGA MAN" with Charlton Heston had resonated with me on a personal level. The symbolic element of a 'lone man' surviving in an apocalyptic world felt oddly familiar, almost as if it were how I perceived my own life in some cinematic dream. I'd always wanted to do my own take on the concept and went to work on a project I called 'HELLTOWN". After completing the screenplay, I decided to do a novelization of it and spent much of my time at the modeling agency, typing away to avoid dealing with the slime ball agents. In the summer of 1990, I finally quit when a new owner took control of the LA office and insisted, I become his personal gopher/lap dog. "F__k you," was the only thing I said before walking out the door, never to return.

Side Note: HELLTOWN" was the first and only screenplay that I'd written that would end up getting optioned. A gentleman named Chris Clifford had a Company called "Crown Village Productions," and he saw the low to moderate budget potential of the script. We became friends and put our efforts into getting the movie made, but our attempts to secure funding were unsuccessful. It just goes to show you how difficult it is to get even an inexpensive film made in Hollywood. It's a wonder anything ever gets produced.

Now in need of employment, I registered with several temp agencies that focused on placing people in the entertainment industry. I'd become extremely 'office proficient' and could handle most anything an executive assistant would be required to handle. Apple One finally called me with an assignment at Buena Vista Home Entertainment (A division of the Walt Disney Company) for one of the Brand Managers who required an assistant for three weeks while her current one took a much-needed vacation.

I worked for a wonderful woman named Patty McInnish, who oversaw all the "Winnie the Pooh" titles for creative services. VHS in 1990 was still in its heyday period, and Disney was king of the hill when it came to Animated titles dominating the market on the format. DVD was still seven years away from its launch, so VHS was the cash cow for Disney, making even more money than the Theme Parks due to consumer demand for the classics.

My brief stint with Patty ended, but the office manager for the department (Phyllis Sawyer) made a call, on my behalf, to the retail division, where they scooped me up to join a team that handled all the video orders from the various retailers.

Target, Walmart, K-Mart, Sears, and many of the other large chains were in constant need of replenishment and could phone into a direct retail hotline where we would take their orders and pass the requests on to the sales reps. It was an easy job that required sitting in a cubicle and waiting for the phone to ring. As there were about 10 of us handling the calls, there was a lot of 'nothing' to do, and I swear I must have read 30-40 paperbacks during the year I spent 'downstairs.'

Disney was famous for hiring temps to fill jobs to avoid paying benefits and other perks that came with being a full-time salaried employee. They were also notorious for having their bean counters crunch numbers and then tell the department heads that they would have to cut costs, which usually meant all the temps got let go. I managed to survive several cuts during the year, but they finally caught up with me around September of 1991.

Without skipping a beat, I called Phyllis to tell her the news and to see if she had anything for me back in creative services. It turned out she did and told me to come up for the details. She needed someone, in a temporary capacity, to serve as an executive assistant for the Vice President of the Department. The job would last as long as it took to find a full-time replacement. I readily accepted the posting and went to work assisting VP Randall Erickson the very next day.

BVHV, as it was known, was not located on the Disney lot. It was relegated to the FAIRMONT Building on the corner of Pass Ave. and Riverside Dr. in Burbank, just a few doors down from the famous original BOB'S BIG BOY restaurant. Except for Disney Character Voices, whose offices were on the first floor, all the other levels were home to BVHV. The Fairmont building was by no means the Ritz Carlton of office buildings. For those of us who worked there, we often referred to it as the Plaguemont Bldg. I'm sure it'd been in use for at least 25 years before I got there and, from what I could tell, hadn't had any restoration or upgrades done to it in all that time.

There were two reasons why we referred to it as "plaguemont'. The first and most egregious were the rats. The Creative Services department was on the 3rd floor of the building's six-floor total. About mid-point on the 3rd floor was a balcony where people went to smoke; yes, smoking was still very much a thing in 1991. The balcony had Bougainvillea crawling all over the walls and railings, which is like crack cocaine to rats. When someone opened the door to go out and puff a few, a rat or two would sneak in and run down the halls past everyone's open office or cubicle. Squeals and yelps erupted as the rat ran and then disappeared to God knows where. It was hilarious. The 2nd reason was related to power outages. It seems a week wouldn't go by without a power outage that would last for hours. When that happened, everyone would get sent home since, without power, the computers were useless. You'd think that a division that was earning more money than any other division in the Company would warrant at least some sort of prestigious office space. But no such luck. I'm guessing the bean counters, once again, had something to do with it.

By early 1992, I was still working for Randy in a temporary capacity, when BVHV finally offered me the position. As I was very comfortable there and the offered salary and benefits were nearly as good as I was making at Drexel, I heartily accepted. I was now officially a Disney employee and part of the creative machine churning out one animated hit after another. But 1992 almost turned out to be my last year on planet Earth.

Carol and I were still living on Rowena in Silverlake when on a Sunday morning, I went outside to clean the windows on Carol's Car. She parked on the street as we only had one carport space, and I kept my Samurai back there. I crossed Rowena and started on the windows, working my way from front to back on the street side of the car. While I was spraying and wiping the driver's side portion of the rear window, I began to feel pressure on the back of my legs, then was immediately pulled down, turned against the car, and dragged along the pavement. I distinctly recall hearing the tires crunching on the asphalt as a blurred image of the rubber rolled inches in front of my face. The whole thing happened so fast I barely noticed that I was now at the front of Carol's car with my back up against the front tire. I could see blood covering my legs, and I kept waiting for the wash of pain to follow, but it never did.

All I could hear was a woman screaming at the top of her lungs, "Oh my God! Oh, my God! What have I done!" The quiet Sunday morning calm had erupted into screams of anguish, bringing a few neighbors out to see what was happening. Carol had heard it and came running only to see me on the ground bleeding in the street. She started screaming back at the woman standing by her car, now stopped in the middle of Rowena.

From what she told Carol, she'd been coming down the side street just behind where Carol's car was parked. She had a can of soda resting on the dash, and when she turned the corner onto Rowena, the can fell off onto the floor. As she bent over to pick it up. The movement caused her to pull the wheel farther into the turn, which pinned me against the back of Carol's Maxima. Her head popped back up just in time to pull the wheel away from the turn, as she instantly realized she'd hit and dragged someone between the two vehicles.

While I sat there numb, quietly assessing my damage, I heard an ambulance arriving. Carol was with me, crying as she looked at the blood covering my right arm and both my legs from the patches of missing skin torn away by the pavement. The EMTs rushed over and went to work on me but were surprised when I suddenly stood up on my own. One EMT told me that it was a complete miracle because he had seen this type of accident many times before, and it always ended in either one of two ways, crushed limbs or death. For me to be standing with no broken bones, and only skin abrasions was a gift from God. "It's one for the books," the other EMT said.

The woman driver had finally calmed down and readily admitted it was all her fault (Duh). Carol took care of getting the necessary License and Insurance information her while the medics finished treating my wounds. They asked me if I wanted to get checked out at the hospital, but I declined, knowing that I was alright. In hindsight, I should have gone as it would have strengthened my claim and provided for a better settlement from her Insurance Company. After a year of repeated phone calls and letters, I wound up receiving a mere six thousand dollars for my brush with death.

As I started to heal, I was fast becoming a permanent fixture at The Colony. I took on ushering duties, assisted with props and set construction, and anything else where an extra set of hands were needed. I'll never forget the first time I went to the Theatre with Carol to see a production of "NAKED DANCING" Directed by Jules Aaron. No, it had no people dancing naked in it, that was just the title. As soon as I walked in, I knew I was home. A Theatre has a scent all its own. The combination of wood, paint, makeup, perfumes, and several other ingredients all combine to create an aroma that I find intoxicating. On one side of the lobby, there was a wall of headshots that showcased all the current members of the Colony's talent roster. As I perused the photos, only one thought went through my mind. I would not rest until my picture was up there as well. I wanted in, in a bad way. I'd gone long enough without feeding my actor's creative appetite and was determined to rekindle the flame. Live Theatre was where it'd all started for me, and I wanted to be wrapped in its comforting embrace again.

BVHV was very understanding after the accident and let me take some time off to recoup from the trauma. But I chose to go back to work after a week as I didn't want to take the chance that they might replace me. However, my concerns were for naught. I'd firmly established myself as part of the team and learned that this team took care of its own.

It wasn't until the summer of 1993 that I finally got around to auditioning for the Colony. It'd taken me that long to get up the nerve to put myself back out there again, and just because Carol was my girlfriend didn't mean there were any guarantees that I'd be worthy enough for membership status. Some big names had graced the Colony's stage over the years before my arrival with John Larroquette and Ed Harris, just two of its members who'd gone on to big success. There was also the matter of my having been away from performing for so long. It'd been 14 years since my last acting job at the age of 21, and I was now 35 years old and no longer the 'kid' with a babyface. I was old enough to have a 'kid' of my own and was severely questioning whether or not I had the chops to perform as an adult. To say I was scared shitless was an understatement. It was a defining moment that would finally answer the question of whether I really had the talent or had just got by being cute and capable. The answer came when The Colony pinned my headshot to the wall, and I fulfilled my wish.

Me at 33.

As with most small Theatres in LA, politics has a big hand on who will get cast and who won't, and the Colony was no exception. I was now the newbie that needed to properly align himself to the pecking order. The first step of becoming a member had been accomplished, but the second step of getting cast in a show would take a little longer. I auditioned for three plays before being cast in a 2nd stage production of "THE FANTASTIKS" in the fall of 1993. My friend Tom Shea from Newington had made his way west a year earlier, and we fell back into our brother-like relationship as if no time had passed at all.

2nd stage productions were quietly referred to as 'Bastard Stepchildren' because they weren't a main-stage production but considered a 'bonus' show for the subscribers. It was a way for the Theatre to raise additional revenue by asking for donations after the show. There were no reviews, and you had to make use of whatever set was currently standing for the main-stage production. It also gave company members an outlet for trying their hand at producing or directing something on their own.

Don Woodruff was our Director, and he decided to 'play' with the character casting just a bit. Instead of it being two fathers whose son and daughter were in love, he opted instead to make the boy's father a mother—the switch up offering a hint of a possible attraction between the parents as well. "The Fantastiks" was always an audience favorite, having had the distinction of being Off-Broadways longest-running musical in history with 42 years and 17,162 performances to its credit. Even to this day, it remains a staple among regional, community, and high school theatres, with approximately 250 new productions mounted each year.

Rachel Sheppard played my daughter, and Tom Shea played the son. Working with Tom for the first time was a blast, and the production ended up a smashing success. It raised more money than any other 2nd stage show before it, setting a record that lasted for many years before finally being surpassed.

I continued to work at BVHV, but Carol had left her job and was now temping wherever there was work available and performing at the Theatre from time to time. At the end of 1993, we decided that we needed more space and found a place in Atwater Village that we liked. It was a house that comprised two apartments, one up and one down. We rented the upper unit because the lower one was already occupied. Carol also decided to get a small dog that she named Casey. Casey was a rat terrier, similar to a Jack Russell terrier but a little taller with pointed ears. I still had Paco, who was now 13 years old but didn't look a day over 8, and the two of them got along just fine.

Our new apartment was just across the street from another member of the Theatre group by the name of Robert O'Reilly. Robert had achieved recognition playing Chancellor Gowron on "STAR TREK: THE NEXT GENERATION and appearing in over a hundred films and television episodes. Robert would ultimately spend ten years as the Klingon leader bouncing his performances between "STNG" and "DEEP SPACE NINE." Robert had been married to Carol's best friend Kim Alexander, but they had divorced shortly before I first met her. At that time, Kim was dating Blaise Bellew, a former race car driver who now worked in the industry as a Chief Electrician for film and stage. Blaise was another guy I made a deep connection with, and we've stayed friends ever since. Today, Blaise is one of my most trusted and valued buddies; his insights and sense of humor make him a treasure, and I am blessed to still have him a part of my life.

Robert was a very cool guy and a very talented actor, so in 1996 when he asked me to be his assistant director on the Colony's production of "MORNINGS AT SEVEN," I jumped at the chance. It ended up proving to be a satisfying creative collaboration and a terrific working experience.

By the summer of 1994, I began to notice some changes in Carol's personality and behavior. She'd started sleeping a lot and was prone to extreme mood swings, crying uncontrollably one moment and then laughing hysterically the next. She'd stopped working and spent most of her time at home painting ornaments and other baubles that she would give as gifts to friends. We hardly ever spoke, and her erratic behavior started taking its toll on our relationship. I wanted to help her find out what was wrong, but she was so irrational that it made any sort of clear communication impossible.

Her Doctor said she was having a nervous breakdown, so I reached out to her mother, Claire, who eventually came and brought her back to her home in Desert Hot Springs. She needed to be continuously monitored, but my work schedule at Disney made it impossible for me to provide her with the vital 24/7 attention she required. I know this sounds like I abandoned her, but that wasn't the case. She'd become fixated on me as her target of choice when the ranting and mood swings took over, so it was decided that I should be taken out of the picture to assist in helping her get better. Both Claire and Carol's Doctor agreed that it would be the best thing for her and for me. It was a sad ending to a relationship that had rescued me in a time of need and given me back a part of my life that I thought was gone forever. Carol had been my muse, and it was how I best chose to remember her at the eulogy held in her honor at The Colony Theatre in 2011 after she passed away from cancer. She'd come to see me at my office late in 2010 to explain that It'd been the early formation of the disease that had caused her irrational behavior and mood swings back in 95'. She expressed her sorrow over how things had ended between us and wanted to see me one last time. It was devastating news and emotional final goodbye.

It was now January of 1995, and work at BVHV was progressing nicely. I moved, yet again, to a one-bedroom apartment on Olive Ave. near Victory Blvd. in Burbank to be closer to the office. I'd managed to stay in touch with Joel Gretsch since leaving the Modeling Agency, and Joel was kind enough to help me move into the new digs.

A few months earlier, at BVHV, plans were getting underway for the release of "GARGOYLES" on VHS. And creative was looking for something unique to add to the release as an added bonus. Gordon Ho was a senior marketing guy from the 6th floor who came up with an idea for a video interactive board game based on the animated series. Everyone knew I was a big comic book and toy aficionado because my cubical always had toys and collectibles on display, so Gordon asked me if I'd like to develop the idea with him. I jumped at the chance to create something that seemed like an impossibility due to the VHS formats analog/linear only capability. DVD would eventually change things up as it was a digital environment that could be programmed to branch out commands in any direction. The game was a challenge that would prove revolutionary if we could create a linear based contest that never played the same way twice.

Both Gordon and I put our heads together and designed a game board that players would traverse while making selections from the on-screen video footage. We chose a pair of dice as the means to determine how many spaces a player could move. It was also the simplest solution to keeping the game random because each roll would offer up a different number. Once you landed on the determined space, you would choose an action card image depicted on the square you landed on. You would either then follow the card's instructions or instructed to 'play' the video to get a different directive. It was a simple and brilliant design. Its inclusion on the release was a huge hit, with reviewers raving about the game's playability despite the linear constraints of the format.

Right around April of 1995, I got a call from HR. They asked to see me and, to my surprise, revealed that my name was on a shortlist of candidates identified as a possible 2nd assistant to the President of BVHV, a woman who was a visionary and had single-handedly revolutionized the home video retail market. She was arguably one of the most valuable executives Disney had and one who had only begun to touch the tip of the iceberg of her accomplishments.

Her 1st assistant arranged the interview, which lasted about 15 minutes. We discussed my time at BVHV so far and my accomplishment working with Gordon Ho. She seemed genuinely impressed with my abilities and ended our meeting by indicating that HR would get back to me soon. I left feeling pretty confident and very impressed with her and her ability to make me feel that my skills were the focus, rather than it being about her and her needs. There was a genuine warmth to her that was a rare attribute when it came to top Executives. Most were cold and dismissive because they were in constant fear of being replaced, so they felt they needed to project an image of 'toughness' to keep everyone at a distance. She was certainly not that type. She didn't need to be because she had enough confidence in herself and those around her to be gracious and sincere. She was the definition of class.

HR called me the next day and offered me the position. My salary would get a nice increase to reflect the stature of working for the Division President, and I would relocate my space to a desk positioned across from her 1st assistant's on the 6th floor. Everyone in the creative services department poked fun at me with comments like, "Ooooh, working for the head honcho, eh? They'll be no living with you now." And "Don't forget us when you end up working for Michael Eisner." It was all in good fun, and I was going to miss the camaraderie we all shared. Creative was home for liked minded people like me. They were artists, writers, designers, and visionaries with wacky personalities to match.

My new boss and her 1st assistant warmly welcomed me as I began my first day in her office, and then we quickly got down to business deciding how best to integrate me into the daily routines. As part of working for a high-level executive, you're required to sign an NDA (Non-Disclosure Agreement). An NDA is your signed agreement with the Company not to disclose any confidential or proprietary information you may become aware of while working for someone that deals with highly classified information. At her level, this type of knowledge was a daily concern due to deals, phone calls, and meetings that were rife in detail that only a handful of people were 'in the know.'

It didn't take long for me to incorporate my abilities into the daily needs of her office. The 1st assistant and I worked well together, and she was very patient during the transition. It wasn't uncommon for her to come out of her office and 'chat' with us and make sure we felt comfortable with the new arrangement. I very quickly grew into becoming protective of both these women as their kindness and work ethic was unparalleled in such a professional/executive environment.

Ann often traveled for meetings and retreats that BVHV would hold at Various locations. Most typically were the retreats that brought all the Senior Execs together for planning, financial reviews, departmental updates, and other strategic mandates that needed implementation. These retreats usually lasted from 3 to 4 days and would be held at a luxury resort Hotel with excellent business meeting and conference room accommodations.

Disney might have scrimped on BVHV's home office digs, but it certainly didn't cut any corners when it came to keeping the execs happy while working hard for the money.

I was still a member of The Colony but had reduced the time I would invest there due to work. My nights were still free; I just chose to remain at home and spend time with Paco, who only got to see and interact with me when I was there. Besides, even though I was a resident member, the Theatre still hadn't afforded me the opportunity to perform on the main stage, and my frustration over all the favoritism and 'clickish' behavior was wearing thin. I was resigned to leaving if I didn't get cast in something soon.

Well, I got cast. In June (1995), The Colony was set to produce a World Premiere production of short stories from renowned Science-Fiction author Ray Bradbury. "THE WORLD OF RAY BRADBURY" showcased stories from "THE MARTIAN CHRONICLES," "THE ILLUSTRATED MAN," and "FAHRENHEIT 451" with a cast of actors performing multiple roles throughout the selections. Ray himself was involved and was there from day one working with the Director and the cast. I was picked to play four roles with my role as 'The Father' in 'The Veldt,' my showcase piece. I was also an Astronaut in "Kaleidoscope" and a 'Drifter' in the "Fahrenheit 451" segment.

"TWORB," as we referred to it, was the most ambitious production The Colony had ever produced. Its Director was the husband of the Theatre's resident Artistic Director, and he used every resource available to him to create sets and special effects that were unheard of on a 99-seat theatre stage. It was a marvel to behold but damn near bankrupted the Theatre. It would take several years before The Colony would recover from the financial hit.

The show was well-received, with reviewers astonished by the creative techniques used to bring the stories to life. Lights, sound, pyrotechnics, RC controlled vehicles, costumes, props, and forced perspectives all combined to bring the audience into the 'Worlds" of Bradbury's imagination. Tickets for the show became so hard to get that a 2-week extension was necessary to fulfill the demand. We'd opened in late August and didn't close until mid-October, nearly four months after starting rehearsals. I even convinced my boss and several other senior staffers to attend. And to my delight, they came and were certifiably impressed with my performance and the production values.

During the run of "TWORB," someone in creative services suggested that I pass by my old desk on the 3rd floor. There was a new employee seated in the cubicle directly next to my old one who they felt I should meet as we had much in common, and she was single. The first chance I had, I went strolling downstairs to get a glimpse of this new team member who sounded so intriguing. I tried to find a reason to slow down and get a good look at her, so I struck up a conversation with the gentleman who had replaced me and was seated in the cubicle next to hers. What I saw was absolutely lovely.

She was not what most people who knew me would call 'my type.' I'd almost always gravitated towards blondes, most likely due to the fact that nearly everyone in my family was a blonde. I guess you stick with what you know.

Her name was Rebecca Hayes, or 'Becky' as she preferred to be called. She was around 5 feet 4 inches tall, with curly dark brown shoulder-length hair and blue eyes. She also had a fantastic physique.

Rebecca Hayes, 1995

It took multiple passes by her cubicle to ascertain this data, and I think after around the 6th, or 7th time, she got suspicious that I was checking her out. I rarely had a reason to be on the 3rd floor unless I was visiting someone I knew or picking up materials for Ann to look over from Randy's office. She would smile each time I came by while I tried to figure out a way to start a conversation without putting my foot in mouth. My informant provided a few more details about her, finally giving me the needed info to introduce myself. She already knew who I was at BVHV because she'd asked other creative services staff, "Who is that guy that keeps walking past my cube?" Stealth was clearly not working for me here.

Part of me was hesitating as it had only been 9 months since the end of my 5-year relationship with Carol. I was actually enjoying my bachelorhood and was a bit reticent at the thought of giving it up. Still, my male hormones overrode my need for solitude, so I initiated my first salvo.

I opened with a "Hi," followed by, "I understand you're an actress. Performing is something we have in common." I then formally introduced myself, and the conversation grew from there. We started emailing each other during the day with silly stuff about Star Trek: TNG, which I was delighted to find out she was a fan of, and other not-work-related nonsense. We talked about getting together outside of work, but "TWORB" was still running, and she was in rehearsals for a production of Horton Foote's "A TRIP TO BOUNTIFUL" at the Actor's Co-Op in Hollywood. We'd have to wait until "TWORB" closed for me to come and see her in 'Bountiful.' Our first official date would end up being the night I came to see her at the Co-Op.

REBECCA & THE ACTOR'S CO-OP:

Becky had arranged a ticket for me with a seat in front row center. The Crossley Theatres location was on the campus of The First Presbyterian Church of Hollywood On Gower between Hollywood Blvd. and Franklin Ave. The Co-Op also had a 2nd space called the Terrace, but its name was later changed to the David Schaal Theatre in honor of the Co-Op's founder, who unexpectedly passed away in 2003.

Like The Colony, The Crossley was part of the 99 seat Theatre waiver contract. This contract meant that both Equity members and non-Equity members could perform there, but the Union (Equity) actors waived payment of the usual Equity contract salary. As the Theatres could only seat 99 people or less, they could not generate enough income to pay both the performers and the production costs associated with running the Theatre space. It was a non-profit type of arrangement that gave actors a venue to be seen, hone their craft, and audiences a less expensive alternative to the more substantial 'Equity only' playhouses like The Pantages, The Dorothy Chandler or the Geffen Playhouse.

The Crossley was still presenting shows in a proscenium format with a 98-seat total but would later change its configuration to a black-box layout to allow for more creative production options. The house was full on the night I attended, with the din of the audience subsiding as the house lights dimmed to black before the stage lights came up. The first thing I saw was Rebecca rising from a bed in her nightgown center stage. At that very moment, I heard a voice, clear as a bell say to me, "You're going to marry this woman." Slowly, I glanced at the people on either side of me and directly behind me to see if they had made the statement. All of them had their focus on the stage with no sign of having said anything. I knew it wasn't my imagination. The words had been too clear as if someone had whispered in my ear. I chose not to give it any more thought and put my attention back to the stage, quickly forgetting about the ghostly prediction.

Rebecca was mesmerizing, and the show was a charming rendition of one of America's premier playwrights. Once again, my heart was captured, but a deeper, more fated connection was yet to come. After the show, we were both hungry, so we made our way over to Little Tony's Pizzeria on Lankershim Blvd. in North Hollywood. It was close to where Becky lived and not far from my place on Olive Ave. We sat and shared a pizza while discussing the play and her stellar performance. Before we parted company, she invited me to dinner at her place the following week, and we set the date.

Upon my arrival at her apartment, I was greeted by her little white Maltese named 'Button.' Button had issues with men but didn't seem to object to my presence at all. A couple of quick barks, and that was it. No muss, no fuss. Becky insisted that he was a good judge of character, so his lack of aggression was an indication that I was a decent person.

As Becky prepared dinner, we continued our conversation from Little Tony's. Neither of us was aware of each other's age or any additional background information, so I told her I had just turned 36 in September. She asked what day, and I said the 3rd. She looked at me for a long moment and then asked, "Are you serious?" "Absolutely," I answered and pulled out my driver's license to prove it. She looked at it and then grabbed her own from her purse. September 3rd, 1950, was the date of her birth, the same as mine only eight years apart. "What are the odds of that?" she queried, "About 365 to 1", I replied. We were both so surprised by the coincidence, and our conversation continued in earnest now that we had made this wonderful discovery.

While Becky was serving dinner, I inquired as to what led her to become an actress. She told me a tale that involved her being in the Circus as a young girl. When she was 17 years old, she left home to join the Sailor Circus in Sarasota, Florida. The Sailor Circus was where young hopefuls would go to train in various disciplines of circus performing, from clowning to animal acts and even the flying trapeze. She chose the trapeze and trained for four years to become an aerialist, capable not only on the trapeze but on the ropes and began her life-long love of elephants as well. She'd been a professional athlete, which explained the remarkable physique she had even then at 44. And yes, once again, I was dating an older woman, and I swear, in every instance, it wasn't intentional. It just worked out that way.

Rebecca, Circus Painting

As she continued her story, she told me how each year the Sailor Circus would present all the new performers via a ringed performance, for both the public and talent scouts. The scouts were looking to fill various spots for traveling Circus's touring the United States. One such scout approached her after the show in need of a Flyer to replace a girl on the Ringling show who was having a baby, and she readily accepted. So, off she went on the Circus train to tour the country for the next seven years with Madison Square Garden always one of the troupes longer stops along the way. OK, this is where it gets weird.

I mentioned earlier that I'd attended the Ringling show at Madison Square Garden in 1973 to which she promptly dropped her fork and said, "Then you saw me. I was there in 1973." We both sat across the table from each other stunned. Sharing the same birthday was one thing but having seen her perform as an aerialist 22 years earlier was beyond belief. If ever two people were fated to meet, it was us. It was a revelation that wasn't just a coincidence; it was destiny.

Like I had done with The Colony, I now became a regular presence at the Co-Op, ushering, house managing, and anything else I could do to help out and provide support. The Co-Op was a faith-based Theatre Company formed in 1987 by a group of Christian actors looking to bring quality plays of hope and redemption to their subscribers. My Christian upbringing was split between my father's strong Catholic rigidity and my mother's gentler Protestant approach to worship. I ended up not adhering to either one but did my best to live my life based on the theory that God was within all of us, allowing us to fellowship with him whenever we felt the need. It didn't necessarily require our presence in Church to have a deep and abiding relationship with the Lord.

At the end of October (1995), my boss was scheduled to attend a BVHV retreat at a resort in Arizona called 'The Boulders.' She and all her senior staff would be in attendance for three days at this luxurious golfers paradise that sat smack in the middle of the Arizona desert.

My boss decided that I should go with her to act as a liaison between the resort and the BVHV home office. It would be a trial run to see how the logistics of my supporting her off-site could improve the flow of information with the home office back in Burbank. My hotel and flight arrangements were made, and a week later, I arrived at the resort.

Working with her and the Senior staff at The Boulders proved to be a rewarding experience for all of us. I found myself falling into 'security' mode whenever we were in public and not cloistered in a conference room. I would always find a way to keep an eye on her, maintaining a discreet distance but still within range if she needed me for something. Although she never said anything, I could tell she liked how I handled myself, and this 'bodyguard' approach would last throughout our tenure together. The best trip I took with her was to London for the exclusive premiere of the live-action version of "101 DALMATIANS." The trip also included a week's worth of meetings held in our Hotel, The Knightsbridge. The 8-hour time difference between London and Los Angeles gave me the daytime hours to go sightseeing, which she encouraged. Later in the day, I would check in with her to see if there were any materials or correspondence that needed to be sent to the home office for distribution, but she almost always said, "Nope," and then either released me or invited me to join the staff for dinner. I came to realize that the whole trip had been a gift rather than an actual work excursion. I could never have afforded something like this, so she used my 'assistant' status to have Disney pick up the expense of bringing me along. It was an unprecedented gesture of gratitude that kept me loyal to her for the next four years.

Becky and I were in the throes of a full-fledged relationship that continued to move along at a decent clip. She'd been married and divorced once before, but I could sense that she was waiting for me to 'pop' the question and solidify our union. I had inadvertently mentioned something about my mother's wedding ring, and that I was holding it for safekeeping until the right woman came along. She had apparently kept this nugget of information close in her mind and mentioned it on several occasions. I eventually got the hint.

It was now October of 1996, and we had been seeing each other for a year. I didn't want to rush things, but I couldn't shake the memory of the mystery voice from the Theatre telling me, 'I was going to marry her.' There was no doubt that I loved her, and the 2 instances of providence we discovered were undeniable proof that we were meant to be together. I grabbed the ring from my jewelry box, stuffed it into my pocket, and drove over to her newly purchased 2-bedroom condo in Valley Village.

She knew that something was afoot since I hadn't planned to come over until later, but I didn't want to reveal my intentions just yet. We sat and talked for a while before she said, "You have it, don't you?" "Have what?" I asked while fighting back a smile. "The ring. You brought the ring, didn't you?" How she knew was beyond me since I'd given no indication that I was close to popping the question. She gave me that, 'do you think I'm that stupid?' look that made me laugh and slowly, very slowly to increase the suspense, I pulled the ring from my pocket.

She tentatively took the ring and began looking it over. The setting was relatively simple, comprised of a gold band with a cluster of diamonds that formed a burst at its center. After acknowledging her approval, she looked at me and stared, waiting for me to say something. For a long while, I just stared back at her. "Will you marry me?" I finally asked. "It's about time." She responded. "Yes, I'll marry you.", was her answer.

A month before the wedding was scheduled, I was riding shotgun in my bosses Porsche as she drove us back to the office from the studio. She asked me if we'd found a location yet, and I told her that the weather was posing a problem for our arrangements, as February was a notorious month for rain in

LA. We really wanted an outdoor wedding but booked a reservation at the Mears Center located on the FPCH campus, where the Co-Op was just in case the wet weather continued. "Why don't you have it at my house?" she asked. "What? Really?" I said. "Sure. We've got the big back yard, and we've had events like this before. Why not?" I couldn't believe what she was offering. "We couldn't possibly impose on you and your husband like that." She smiled and then turned a corner. "It's not an imposition, you need a place, and we have one. End of story," "Only if it doesn't rain." I offered back. "Deal." She said and pulled into the garage of the big new building that BVHV had finally moved to.

On February 15th, 1997, Becky and I were married in a ceremony held at my boss's house located in the Hollywood Hills directly above the American Film Institute. In fact, the guest parking for the event was AFI's campus parking lot! And her neighbors were Brad Pitt and Jennifer Aniston, whose home was about 3 houses away! Her 1st assistant had volunteered to be our wedding coordinator, and she did a masterful job of putting all the pieces of the nuptial puzzle together.

We chose a 1940's theme for the occasion where all the guests came dressed in 40's attire, and the entertainment was provided by our friends from the Actor's Co-Op. The Co-Op had recently produced "THE 1940's RADIO HOUR," a reenactment of a radio show from the period, complete with Orchestra, songs, commercials, and radio plays. Once the guests had sat down with their buffet plates, the show got underway.

My soul brother Alex was my best man, and Becky's best friend, Brenda Ballard, was her maid of honor. At one point during the ceremony, we heard a gasp come from some of the guests. Since our backs were facing those in attendance, we couldn't see the two butterflies that had suddenly appeared and danced around us as we spoke our vows. It was yet another sign that our union was blessed.

The happy couple, circa 2006

Another blessing came in the form of generous gifts given by many of the senior staff from BVHV who were in attendance. Before the wedding, the Senior Vice President and my bosses second in command had thrown me a bachelor party at an upscale restaurant in Burbank. The VP of Finance presented me with a cart loaded with Star Trek action figures, ships, and other Trek-related items. It was a total surprise and another testament to the impact I had on the staff while working with her.

Due to work and other commitments, we chose not to take a honeymoon right away. One of several gifts we received from my boss and her husband (along with the use of their home) was an overnight stay on our wedding night at The Four Seasons Hotel on Beverly Drive and Olympic Blvd. Becky and I ran home to take of Button and a second dog named Lily. Lily was a Shih Tzu who we purchased to be a companion for Button and quickly became the 2nd love of my life. We changed clothes and turned over the four-legged kids to our neighbor, who was kind enough to watch them for the night. We had a lovely room with a huge hot tub and....... the rest is personal.

Jeffrey Katzenberg had left Disney at the end of 1994 due to issues he'd had with Michael Eisner and partnered with Steven Spielberg and David Geffen to form DREAMWORKS SKG. Contractual mandates prohibited him from 'poaching' talent from Disney after his departure, but that didn't stop him from finding ways around the directive to bring choice executives over to the new venture. My boss was one of them.

Studios rarely, if ever, took legal action when an Executive jumped ship to another competitor. It happened so frequently and cost too much time and money to pursue. Contracts had loopholes, and often a simple change of job title would be enough to satisfy the former employer's non-competition clause. You'd have to really piss someone off before you left to get the lawyers involved.

Side Note: It was around this time that my father's girlfriend Harriet suffered a stroke. From this point on, she would be relegated to a wheelchair forcing my father to become a full-time caregiver. His limited ability to come and go freely would keep him from spending time at the Saratoga and impose a lengthy period of sobriety on him. We would see each other on occasion, but he remained mostly on his own.

DREAMWORKS:

In June of 1997, my boss announced her departure from Disney to DreamWorks, where her new position was Head of Feature Animation.

Upon her exit, the gentleman who was the President of BVHV International was tasked with merging the Domestic and International business units into one larger division. He already had his own support staff, but my bosses 1st assistant had knowledge of all the BVHV Domestic key players and departments that made her a valuable commodity. I, on the other hand, was considered excess baggage, so he did his very best to try and dump me on some other department. My boss, however, had no intention of leaving me behind. She simply needed to wait until she was settled in at DreamWorks before telling him that she'd be bringing me over.

She knew I had a good working knowledge of Animation and Anime, which might prove helpful in her new position. She also knew that my familiarity with the BVHV staff would come in handy once she started campaigning for talent. Katzenberg was really after her retail marketing skills in the Home Entertainment arena as DW was going to have set up an aftermarket division to release their films once they'd completed their theatrical runs.

A deal was cut with Universal to handle all the mastering and distribution requirements to get the product into stores. At the same time, a new 'Home Entertainment' division was developed by my boss. As soon as I got there, we hit the ground running, formulating the business plan and identifying the needed staffing requirements. "THE PRINCE OF EGYPT" was in pre-production at this time, so my bosses time was divided between familiarizing herself with the project, meeting with the various animation department heads, and devising the Home Entertainment pipeline. It was a busy time, but really exciting as this was DreamWorks in its infancy, and we all knew we were lucky to be a part of something historic.

The formal DreamWorks studio in Glendale was in the midst of construction, so our 'working' offices were located on the backlot of Universal Studios. A nondescript three-story building just off Barham Blvd where Forest Lawn Drive ended served as our temporary home thanks to Spielberg's ties to the studio. His AMBLIN offices had already been a permanent fixture on the lot since 1984, so Universal was more than happy to provide him with additional office space needed to get DreamWorks off the ground.

The whole environment was like a College campus. Nobody kept their doors closed, and everyone was on a first-name basis. It wasn't at all uncommon for Jeffrey or Steven to just pop in to say 'Hi' and see what we were up to. It was just so damn cool to be there. Unfortunately, everything changed when we finally moved into the Actual DreamWorks Studio complex.

The advent of multiple buildings situated on a beautiful Tuscan like setting now put distance between departments and business units that had previously been lumped together in one neat little building. Suddenly office size, location, and window/no window pettiness reared its ugly head as Executives and artists alike vied for space best befitting their perceived stature. Nameplates went up, and doors closed for self-imposed privacy. Assistants now became gatekeepers intent on scheduling meetings instead of allowing the free form impromptu approach presented before the move. It was a beautiful campus, and the cafeteria that provided gourmet delights throughout the day was a terrific perk. Still, we'd sacrificed the 'start-up' innocence for the harsh reality of studio politics. It was inevitable, but it would have been nice to hang onto the feeling for just a little while longer.

In the latter part of 1996, A new video delivery format launched that would change the way we watched media at home in a gigantic way. DVD (Digital Versatile Disc) would revolutionize the Home Entertainment market and propel me forward on a new career path I would never have expected.

VHS was effectively done and dying a slow death. DVD's superior picture and audio qualities were usurping the old format by leaps and bounds and would facilitate the eventual transition of all analog broadcasts to High-Definition. Warner Bros. Studios initially drove the launch with all the other studios following suit by the end of 1997, except DreamWorks. My boss felt there were still some viability and content protection issues that needed to be addressed before DW would release anything on the format. Once the concerns had been tackled, DW signed on and began to prepare their first finished films for release.

Once we moved to the physical animation studio in Glendale, I spoke with her regarding my future at DW's. I was just shy of forty and knew that continuing as an assistant was not something I wanted to do forever. She and I were contemporaries, so she understood my desire to excel beyond the limitations of a support role. I agreed to continue working for her in my current capacity for one more year with the caveat that there would be something else for me at the end of the commitment. She accepted my terms, and we continued on through the release of "THE PRINCE OF EGYPT, and "ANTZ," along with DW's first live-action films that included "THE PEACEMAKER," "AMISTAD," "MOUSEHUNT," and "PAULIE."

The year passed quickly, and she and I sat down again to discuss my options. She arranged for me to meet with several department heads, but my lack of experience combined with the lengthy production time of animation meant it could take years to make any real career strides. But DW's commitment to DVD was about to change everything.

I'd always been an early adopter of technology, and DVD certainly qualified as new technology. I'd investigated and schooled myself on the format's capabilities when it first launched, and my boss knew it. I'll never forget the day she came back to the office from a meeting and called me into her office. "I got it!" she exclaimed. "You're going to help us produce our product for DVD!" I was speechless. Before I knew it, I was being moved to my own office across campus, where Home Entertainment was located, becoming part of a two-man team tasked with making DW's DVDs the Benchmark of the format! It was an extraordinary opportunity and one that would lead to Awards and, eventually, DVD Guru status on the Web.

The expectations from DW were high because of Spielberg and Katzenberg's creative track records. My partner was the head of DW's Animation mastering, and we knew we had to develop designs and content that would knock the socks off both the other studio offerings and consumer expectations. Our first releases set the standard that every other studio now had to achieve, and when the release of "THE PRINCE OF EGYPT" hit the market, we ruled the format. My boss couldn't have been more delighted, but the next two releases were going to prove to be even more significant challenges.

"SAVING PRIVATE RYAN" was a monumental success both critically and financially, winning numerous awards and taking the top spot for the domestic box office in 1998. This was Spielberg at his best, and we had to treat its DVD release with the same care and reverence that Steven had given the films creation. This meant that Steven would be involved, and my partner and I would have to meet with him to get his approval. One such meeting took place at his office at Amblin. My partner had created a bonus segment meant to honor all those who had fought and died on Omaha beach that fateful day of June 6th, 1944. The piece was a simple crawl of names against a black background, with each name identified by what Battalion or Division they represented. Music from John Williams's score played for the duration of the crawl until the screen went black. It was a sobering and emotional presentation that illustrated the enormous loss of life given to protect our freedom.

Steven and his longtime lawyer arrived, and we stepped into his conference room where there was a monitor and DVD player. We all stood silently while Steven watched the segment. When it finished, he mentioned how touching it was and asked where the list of names had come from. My partner indicated it'd been provided by the armed forces from their archive of records made after the war. Steven's attorney also agreed that it was a powerful presentation, but it needed to be 100% accurate to be presented. The intention was admirable, but It would be disheartening for any family who lost someone and didn't find their name on the list. Steven thanked us for our efforts, and the meeting was adjourned. It wasn't the outcome we'd hoped for, but we felt we'd done justice to the material and shown Steven that we were on the right track.

The 2nd release that was going to require some creative thinking was "AMERICAN BEAUTY." The film hadn't yet been released in theaters, but director Sam Mendes wanted to get a head start on what bonus content might be included with the DVD release. A private screening of a workprint was set up for me at the Amblin screening room where I sat, alone with a life-size Raptor prop from 'Jurassic Park' right behind me! The rough-cut I viewed only had a temporary music track from Thomas Newman's score for "THE SHAWSHANK REDEMPTION." Newman was still scoring 'AB,' so the temp tracks were used in their place, and it worked. I was blown away by the film. The direction and the performances were mesmerizing, and I couldn't wait to meet with Sam and discuss his ideas for the disc.

A week later, a meeting was set up to meet with Sam at his office in Santa Monica. Sam was British and a fascinating guy. He had a quiet demeanor and was very passionate about his work. Steven had approached him after being impressed by his stage productions of "OLIVER" and "CABARET" in London. DW's had purchased the "AMERICAN BEAUTY" script from Alan Ball and thought it would be an excellent project for Sam to make his feature film directing debut.

Sam was full of all sorts of ideas for bonus content, but the one that struck us the most was something that would have really been a coup. It was a segment that was shot but ultimately decided against using for the end of the film. It was something fans would have loved to see, but Sam felt that to include scenes he eventually chose not to use would detract from the film's integrity.

It was a solid reason and showed how honest he wanted to remain to the material by not altering it just for 'added value.'

As it turned out, I never had the chance to finish working on "AMERICAN BEAUTY" or "GALAXY QUEST' because I ended up leaving DreamWorks to accept a position as Vice President of DVD at Complete Post in Hollywood.

My partner and I had produced 13 titles on the format and had become DVD producing celebrities on the web. There'd been in-depth interviews with various DVD Review sites, and we'd even participated in one of the web's first podcasts detailing our work on "SAVING PRIVATE RYAN." We'd both won 'Telly' and 'Axiem' awards for our producing efforts and had, much to the studio's surprise, become the voice of DreamWorks Home Entertainment on the internet. We were the team to beat with every studio looking to see what we would come up with next.

It was through my friend Rob Hummel at DreamWorks that I landed at Complete Post. Rob was Head of Animation Technology and oversaw the building of the digital infrastructure for the studio, so he had a lot of clout in the post-production arena of the industry. Complete post was a premiere post house located at Sunset Blvd and Gower. With additional space across the street inside the Gower-Gulch studios. Rob had been there for a meeting when CP's President asked him if he knew anyone who could take over their DVD pre-mastering department. Rob immediately mentioned my name because of the work I had done at DW's where Rob had been one of my biggest supporters. He was always amazed at what we had put together and inspired us to outdo ourselves with every new release. Rob made a huge impact on my career, and even today, I hold in the highest regard as a pioneer in digital cinema technology.

I received a call from the CP President a few days after Rob had dropped my name, and we set up a lunch date to talk. It was flattering to be considered, but I had some reservations about leaving the safety of the studio for a position as a vendor. Studios were the boss, but they relied on vendors to do a lot of the production and post-production heavy lifting. The studio would provide the content, but it was up to whichever vendors they'd hired to produce the final mastered product. If something went wrong or the studio was unhappy with the result, they might fire the vendor and refuse to pay for the services they provided. It also meant that whoever was in charge of the work would likely lose their job as well. It was a slippery slope and a cutthroat business where most people who worked in it wanted 'IN' to the studios where the money and control was. It was exceedingly rare for someone to step 'OUT' of its embrace and into the lion's den.

COMPLETE POST:

CP offered me the job based on my track record and Rob's glowing recommendation. I'd been in the studio environment for 8 years and made some decent progress working my way up the ladder, but any real financial gain would likely take another 8 years, and by that time, I'd be fifty years old. Rebecca and I still had our sights set on owning a home rather than a condo, but our combined salaries weren't enough yet to handle a more expensive mortgage. My DW's salary got a bump in 1997 when I moved over to Home Entertainment but had only moved up slightly during the past eighteen months. CP offered me a VP title and a six-figure salary to come on board, two things that would be out of reach at the studio for the foreseeable future. In the end, the money and title would win out over my need to play it safe. My boss accepted my notice with gracious good luck and wished me well in my new endeavor. It was a career decision that would prove to be both a blessing and a curse.

CP had a DVD pre-mastering department located in the basement of the main Gower-Gulch building on North Gower Street. There were two executive offices just to the right of the reception area, one project manager's office half a floor down, and four mastering bays, one of which was a QC suite. There was also a client viewing room with state-of-the-art playback equipment just across from my office.

The office next to mine was occupied by the Sales VP, who'd arrived six months before I did. He was an easy-going guy whose relaxed manner and comfortable presence served him well when getting potential clients to bring us titles for pre-mastering. He'd put together a decent stable of independents with the occasional studio title thrown in for good measure. The department was surviving but could do better. We worked well together and quickly became friends as well as colleagues. I had some trouble at first with one of the authors (the computer programmer who creates the navigation for the disc). This young man had some authority issues and felt he knew better than everyone else. I'd been warned about him when I arrived, so I was prepared for an attitude, which I got the first time we met. I wasn't used to being in charge, but I also wasn't going to take any crap from someone too big for their britches. I told him to either be a team player or take a walk. There were plenty of other programmers out there who would love to take his seat. He backed down and managed to last about six more months before parting ways with us.

That left us with only one programmer, and it seemed that almost all 'authors,' as they preferred to be called, had an attitude. They indeed had the most complex job in pre-mastering, keeping track of all the various compressed data streams and the connective pathways that linked it all together. But it was hardly an excuse to behave as if without them, you were S.O.L. They were, however, correct in that assumption. Without a talented author, all you had was a whole lot of data with no cohesive links to make it all work. They were, in fact, the glue that held everything together.

We did some excellent work the first ten months I was in charge, and the non-DreamWorks titles offered me a chance to stretch my creative chops by working on films that were more genre-related and dark by comparison. We produced Brian DePalma's "SISTERS" in early 2000 and a special limited edition of Lucio Fulci's "THE BEYOND" released by Anchor Bay in October of the same year. David Cronenberg's "DEAD RINGERS" and Tarsem Singhs "THE CELL" were also on tap along with all the "BENJI" movies. Earlier in the year, I'd designed the menus and supervised the Director's commentary for Showtime's "RATED-X," directed by Emilio Estevez, that starred both Emilio and his brother Charlie Sheen. For the commentary, I decided to have the brothers sit on a couch we'd brought into the sound studio and view the film on a large screen TV. The idea was to get them to feel like they were watching at home, creating a more relaxed environment allowing them to be candid and loose with their comments. They shared a couple of beers together during the session, which made for some lively brotherly banter and the finished disc turned out great.

One really cool and flattering thing that happened during this first year was a call I received from LUCASFILM. Rebecca and I had just arrived at her brother's condo at Kaanapali beach on the island of Maui. We were taking a week's vacation and looking forward to just relaxing on the beach when the call came. They had tracked me down through CP and were interested in discussing their upcoming DVD release of "THE PHANTOM MENACE." My award-winning work at DreamWorks and 'Guru' status on the internet had put me on their radar. They told me that there were only two DVD producers they were considering to design the interface and content for the release, and I was one of them. Van Ling was the other.

The date of the presentation was the day after I got back from vacation, so that meant I'd have to coordinate all of my needed creative materials with the CP art department from Maui! I accepted the challenge and spent the next 2 days working from a business center located in the Hotel next to her brother's condo. While Becky sat on the beach and went sightseeing, I was immersed in creating and planning the details of the disc. A breakdown of potential bonus material and presentation boards illustrating the menu designs and navigational transitions all had to be put together back in LA and ready for my final approval on arrival. I could have declined since I was on vacation, but the honor and prestige of having even been considered dictated that I make the sacrifice.

I spent about 12 hours in total between writing and dictating my creative concepts to the design team back home. Computer capabilities were not as sophisticated in 2000 as they are today, so I was limited by what the team could send me and what would have to wait until I got back. I knew my chances were slim because Van Ling was an actual digital designer capable of fully rendering graphics that would present far better than my static boards. And that would ultimately prove to be the case. Van presented a much more visually complete environment, so he was awarded the job. I didn't mind. I'd made a valiant effort and felt good about what I'd accomplished from a distance on such short notice.

Unbeknownst to me, CP's top management had been negotiating with Technicolor about acquiring the DVD pre-mastering department. There was a 'boys' club that existed in the vendor community that I was not, or ever would, become a part of. These guys all played golf together, their kids went to the same schools, and they kept each other informed on all the back-door deals being discussed by the various post houses. Because I came from a studio, I was considered 'persona-non-grata' and not to be trusted with such inside information. It took only a couple of weeks before both my VP of sales and myself were told we were being let go.

I was furious. CP had gone out of its way to entice me to leave the safety of the studio, and now, one year later, was cutting me loose! I sure as hell wasn't going to go crawling back to DreamWorks with my tail between my legs and listen to everyone tell me, "I could have told you so." I needed a plan, and I needed it fast.

CINESITE:

Ruth Scovill had been the Head of Technology at DreamWorks while I was there, and like Rob Hummel, had been a big fan of the work I was doing. She was a voice of reason and a trusted friend who, shortly after my departure, had also left the comfort of studio life for a role in vendor-vendor land.

Ruth was now President of Cinesite, an award-winning Visual effects division of KODAK. We'd spoken on several occasions about how DVD could play a part in VFX pre-visualization and DVD Dailies for client review purposes. So, Ruth immediately came to mind as Cinesite would be an ideal place to offer pre-mastering capabilities, provided I could convince her of the financial benefits it could bring if we brought our client base with us.

I met with her at the Cinesite offices in Hollywood and made my pitch, which included building an entirely new DVD pre-mastering facility to accomplish the work. As a testament to her faith and trust in me, she said yes and allotted about half a million dollars to the design and build-out of a new operation. Available space at their film vaults (PRO-TECH) in Burbank was provided to us, and we got underway. It would take about 3 months for the offices, tech-bays, equipment, and wiring requirements to be completed before we were up and running. And true to his word, my sales VP had clients already in the wings, ready to make use of our services. Five of us from CP stayed together to comprise Cinesite DVD as it was now called, and I hired a new programmer to finish off the roster.

There was one staff member from CP that stayed with me through Cinesite and New Media, who I must take a moment to recognize here. His name is Craig Rudnick. Craig was the highlight of my time at CP and was, by far, the best QC technician in the business. Craig's love of film and attention to detail was only surpassed by his ability to elicit tears of laughter from me with his impressions and comedic antics. He was the funniest guy I ever knew, and loyal to a fault. We still communicate from time to time, and I'd like to thank him for being a good friend and a loyal employee. It was an honor and a pleasure to work with you. You made all the hard times easier to handle.

I'd given up my VP title in favor of 'Creative Director' as Cinesite already had too many VP's in its roster, but I didn't see it as a demotion. My creative design and content skills were what kept our clients coming back, and the new title made them feel even more assured that I was maintaining a hands-on approach. Showtime continued with us providing titles such as Armistead Maupin's 'TALES OF THE CITY" and the controversial "QUEER AS FOLK" series. And we continued doing a slew of Horror genre titles for several independents. We actually started turning a profit pretty quickly and would have continued to grow if not for September 11, 2001.

The disaster of the Twin Towers in NY put everything on hold with VFX houses taking a hit because studios were now rethinking and scraping projects that featured explosive mass death and destruction. Without the revenue from these big VFX jobs, Cinesite was doomed. It also meant we were now in jeopardy as well.

NEW MEDIA:

According to Ruth, Kodak had never sold a division of theirs in the Company's entire history. But because we were actually turning a profit, they would make an exception and allow Cinesite DVD to be sold if a buyer could be found. I found two potential buyers almost overnight and put them in touch with Ruth to see if they could cut a deal. One of them dropped out immediately, but the 2nd, a digital design and graphics company called New Media, stepped up and made the deal.

Two young men were the co-owners of New Media, and I had called them to see if they were interested. We had worked together before, so I thought adding pre-mastering to their arsenal of services might give them an edge over the other design firms. My only concern was that these two guys were 'young Turks,' and their drive to succeed could sometimes come across as cocky and dismissive. In my opinion, they were talented but rough around the edges.

New Media's offices were located about 20 mins from Pro-Tech, which meant that we'd have to relocate the entire facility from Burbank to their space and rewire everything to integrate the two systems. As this was just before the Christmas holiday of 2002, we used the seasonal downtime to complete the transition. It took a month to get things up and running, and by mid-January of 2003, we were able to start producing titles.

For reasons I won't go into here, things reached a head at New Media in late August, and I decided to part company with them. I'd grown tired of working for other people and wanted to open my own facility. I was pretty sure I could manage it if I played my cards right. It would be a big commitment, but it's what I felt I needed to do.

MONARCH DIGITAL SERVICES:

One month after I left New Media, I secured a $250,000.00 startup loan from the bank that Becky and I had our home mortgage with. The amount was half of what Cinesite had allotted for a similar buildout. So, it would take some very creative thinking and deal-making to acquire the proper space and equipment needed to make MDS a reality. It was, however, my good fortune to have made the acquaintance of a young technical visionary by the name of David Schultens. David had worked for me before at New Media when I needed additional help getting the equipment room and cabling installed. So, I reached out to him again with the challenge of putting together a cutting-edge digital pipeline for just pennies on the dollar.

David was well connected and knew all the equipment vendors willing to cut deals if 'cash' was an option. Within weeks we'd acquired nearly all the hardware, leaving only the two most expensive items on our list to negotiate a purchase. The software used to compress all the video data and the programming system used to manage all the discs navigation weren't cheap, but once again, David managed to work his magic and secure what we needed for a fraction of the cost. It's how he earned his nickname of 'Gandalf.'

While David was busy digital dumpster diving, I was busy putting together a team that could operate everything. My first hire for the role of office manager was Rick Johnson. I'd already known Rick for a few years as he had eventually taken over as Randy Erickson's assistant at Disney. Rick was also a past performer and had done work at The Colony before I'd gotten involved. Rick and I were kindred spirits who both suffered in silence from the same psychotic insecurities and self-doubts that had plagued us all our lives. It was like we were one mind sharing two bodies, but our Borg Collective connection actually worked because we didn't need to speak to know what the other was thinking.

There were now three of us, and I still needed 3 more to fill the technical spots of compression, authoring, and QC. Michael Malooly had been my compression master at CP, Cinesite, New Media, and, hopefully, MDS. Like Craig, Mike was a trusted and loyal friend and employee. He was also really good at what he did. One phone call from me and Michael was on board. One down, two to go.

My next staffer came from a DVD facility just down the street from the MDS offices. When looking for space, I was determined to find a location central to the studios and independents we worked with. My search didn't take long when I found office space in the old Dick Clark bungalows on Olive Ave. in Burbank. We were flanked on either side by NBC Studios to our south and the new Dick Clark offices to our north. We had a business office on the 2nd floor and a large open space suite on the 1st floor at the back of the building. The downstairs suite had one small private office that we used for QC, with the remainder of the space taken up with equipment and workstations. There was even an area with a wall screen that became a 'screening room' area for clients and a place for us to hang out as a group and take meetings. The whole thing was very bohemian with wires and conduit everywhere lit by glowing monitors and machine control lights of every color. As long as the lights were down, everything looked like the inside of a spaceship. But turn up the lights, and the hidden chaos was visibly crawling everywhere.

Dan McKeaney came on board as our new author, who proved to be a valuable asset despite his penchant for resisting David's requests, occasionally rubbing Mike the wrong way, and my desire for him to be a team player. Dan was a bit of a 'goth' who marched to his own beat, but there was no denying his talent. He pulled us out of the fire many times with his creative solutions and willingness to work at all hours. He gave me his best, and I always respected him for it. The last position I needed to fill was for QC, and I'd hoped to convince Craig to join us. His presence and QC acumen were much needed, but alas, it wasn't meant to be. Craig wanted the stability of an established facility that offered job security. We were a startup with limited backing and no guarantee of continued success. I couldn't argue with his rationale but wished he'd been able to trust in my ability to build something he should have been a part of.

MDS had a soft opening in November of 2003 with an official opening in January of 2004. I would have to handle new client pitches until we could find someone with potential contacts to drive sales. We didn't have the money to pay a salary, so it would have to be somebody willing to work on commission. Not an ideal solution, but it was the only one we had. Of course, it would take Gandalf to come through again and provide us a fellow he knew named Jim Stanton to accept the terms and join our motley crew. Jim was a quirky guy who had a tendency to talk too much and get on everybody's nerves. He meant well and managed to make some solid contacts, but never really delivered any concrete clients. I liked Jim. I just didn't think he was cut out for sales.

Once we were up and running, work began in earnest on titles from Freemantle Media such as "THE BEST AND WORST OF AMERICAN IDOL: Seasons 1-4", "FOOTBALLER'S WIVES," "JAMIE'S KITCHEN," and "COUNT DUCKULA: The complete first season." New West Records gave us about 18 "LIVE FROM AUSTIN CITY LIMITS" concerts to go along with work from Disney that I'd managed to secure. David even became a consultant to Bruckheimer Productions, working with their editors and mastering teams to educate them on the needed parameters required for Blu-ray releases. We did trailers for "PIRATES OF THE CARRIBEAN: CURSE OF THE BLACK PEARL" and "POTC: DEAD MAN'S CHEST." We even did a promo disc for Pontiac's launch of the *Solstice* Sports car.

The real trial by fire that proved the quality level of work we could provide came when CRITERION approved us as a vendor. CRITERION was known industry-wide as the most demanding release company in the format. Any pre-mastering facility they considered was required to provide compression segments supervised by one of their in-house producers. Every detail of picture clarity, black levels, pixelization, and other potential hazards were scrutinized. If a problem was found and couldn't be rectified immediately, you were out. Thanks to Michael Malooly's deft skills, we passed muster and produced two titles for them. It was a badge of honor that very few facilities could proudly display.

In 2001 while I was at Cinesite, Becky and I'd finally purchased a home in Sherman Oaks. It was a beautiful 3500 sq.ft. 4 bedroom 3 ½ bath cottage style with a pool and spa. Becky adored it, and for me, it became a sign of just how far I'd come since losing everything in 1985. On paper, I was now officially a millionaire and praised God for getting me through the tough times. Life was good, but it wouldn't last for long.

With Rosie, Button, Lil' Red, Lily, and Paco, circa 2008

I had to borrow heavily against the house to make payroll as less and less work came our way. The big guns like Technicolor and Deluxe started offering the same type of services we provided to our clients for free to secure their replication business. The profit margins on replication were so great that offering a free $30,000.00 pre-mastering job (the work we did) was nothing compared to hundreds of thousands of dollars made from replicating the mastered product. We had no way to compete with this, so MDS and a host of other smaller digital service facilities were forced to close their doors for lack of work. It was akin to what happened when Walmart opened a store near communities where prosperous small businesses suddenly found themselves out of business due to the massive retailer's volume pricing and one-stop shopping.

The DVD industry had changed over its 1st ten years, shifting from using thriving open-market cottage facilities to big profit margined industry powerhouses. MDS managed to keep its doors open until June of 2007 when finances both personally and business-wise reached rock bottom. The most challenging day of my life was having to let everybody go and to try and figure out what my next move would be.

LIFE AFTER DEATH:

Misery loves company, and this time instead of facing the future alone, I had Rebecca at my side. Despite everything, Becky was still there, still holding my hand and hopeful that things would work out. I was blessed with a good woman who chose not to bail at the first sign of trouble and who supported me through all of it. We'd been to hell and back together, and the experience had made our bond even more vital. We needed each other now more than ever, and I was determined to keep her faith in me intact.

Something exciting happened just before MDS closed. In April, Becky auditioned for a role at the Sierra Madre Playhouse for a production of "ANGEL STREET." I tagged along with her for support, but when we arrived, the Director asked if I was an actor and if I'd be willing to read for the male lead. I was shocked, but Becky said, "Go for it." I hadn't done any theatre since TWORB at the Colony, which was 12 years back, but I thought 'what the hell' and read for him. He cast me but not Becky, and I was mortified that I had unintentionally stolen her thunder. She was completely fine with the outcome and was as supportive as I could possibly have hoped.

Rehearsals started right away, and we opened about 4 weeks later. I relished every minute of it and, at the age of 49, felt that I'd finally outgrown my baby-faced image and become the adult actor I'd always known I could be.

I would be remiss if I didn't mention the friendship I'd found with a gentleman who was our neighbor in Sherman Oaks. The story of Michael J. Corgnati is a lengthy one and worthy of an entire book all its own. Michael and I became very close and remained the best of friends until his untimely passing in 2017. For many years before we'd met, he'd had a successful career as a commercial producer and idea man. Mike was chock full of stories about Hollywood and the programs he'd produced and had a natural charm that wasn't phony or forced. I can honestly say that I loved Michael for his compassion and selflessness, which were such rare commodities in

LA. He had the patience of a saint and deserved so much more from life then what he was ultimately given. I miss him more and more as each day goes by.

SONY:

In September of 2008, I turned 50. Becky was still plugging away at Disney, but the closure of MDS meant I was no longer earning a salary. I was collecting unemployment, but we were in debt up to our ears and unable to pay the mortgage, the business loan, or the 2nd I'd taken to cover payroll. The bank began to make threats, and we were forced into filing for bankruptcy. By March of 2009, the BK was finalized, but I was still unemployed. I found it ironic that I was now too old and overqualified to secure a position in the world of DVD that I'd been such a driving force in for the past 10 years.

I finally managed to land a position at SONY. SONY already had a sizeable pre-mastering facility located on their studio lot in Culver City but wanted to build a 2nd smaller one in Century City. My background and supervision experience in the build-out of three previous operations made me the ideal candidate to assist in their needs. I was confident I'd found a new home and that our financial troubles would be put to rest, but SONY and I would prove to be a bad fit.

As a corporation, SONY did things via process' that slowed progress down to a crawl. Every effort made to secure a vendor or a piece of equipment was met with a wall of red tape. Multiple bids were required for everything and had to be run through numerous departments before even being considered. I'd brought David along to assist me, but we couldn't even purchase a piece of software without spending two days trying to convince someone why we needed it!

I'd assembled state of the art facilities by the seat of my pants, and SONY couldn't even get out of its own way to allow us to do the job. After 3 months of making zero progress, SONY and I parted company. There is such a thing as too much oversight, and Disney had often been accused of it. SONY, however, broke the mold and took it to all new heights.

The Actor's Co-Op still remained a large part of both Becky's and my life, and I finally decided that it was high time I became a full-fledged member. When the new member auditions were held later that year, I found myself accepted with open arms by the entire company. It proved to be a blessing in so many ways by giving me the opportunities to work creatively with my wife and embrace my newfound confidence as a mature actor, who'd finally outgrown the self-imposed stigma of being a child performer.

DAD:

As I mentioned earlier in this tale, my father had become a full-time caregiver to Harriet after her stroke. With only their combined social security and her disability as income, the barhopping had come to a grinding halt. From her stroke in 1998 to her death in 2009, my father didn't drink. Almost 11 years of self-imposed sobriety to care for a woman I hardly even knew. It was a hard pill for me to swallow. I kept thinking that if he'd only applied that same commitment to his marriage, things might have turned out a whole lot different for all of us.

I'd long since given up on laying blame and found some middle ground with him during his sobriety. He was an OK guy when he wasn't drinking, and we could actually hold a conversation without arguing. Deep down, I could sense that he was really proud of my accomplishments and how I'd managed to turn a series of adverse life-changing events into ones with positive and beneficial outcomes. He never actually said it out loud, but there were times I could see the smile in his eyes. It was the most I could ever hope for from him.

During the intervening years of his sobriety, he was fitted with a stint in one of his groin arteries. For some reason, the blood flow during the surgery was left off for too long, resulting in kidney damage. When he awoke afterward, his doctor told him that he would require regular sessions of dialysis. Somehow, and even his doctor didn't know why, he remained stable enough to never need a single session. I told him how lucky he was and not to tempt fate by going back to the booze. He'd been sober for so long; it shouldn't be that difficult to continue his abstinence. Besides, his damaged kidneys couldn't handle it now like they once did. My plea for self-control fell on deaf ears when no sooner did Harriet pass on; he began drinking again. At first, it was just beer, but the hard liquor quickly followed.

Next came a diagnosis of colon cancer, which was removed, followed by freezing a section of his prostate also due to cancer. He was 80 years old and still hadn't learned anything from his mistakes or his behavior. Despite all this, he could always be found seated every day at the bar at Ireland's 42 or the Robin Hood on Burbank Blvd.

Harriet's death also meant the end of her social security and disability payments. I'd told him numerous times to just get married to ensure he'd continue to receive her income, but he just flat out refused. His SSI was not enough for him to pay rent, so it forced me into having him come live with us at the house. Becky didn't like him, and his dismissive 'know-it-all' attitude rubbed her the wrong way daily. His presence was driving a wedge between us that I never thought could happen.

One morning I went downstairs to check on him because it was unusual for him not to be up and out by 11:00am. His room was actually a spare bedroom next to the laundry room. I knocked on the door and heard a faint, muffled groan then immediately opened the door to find him sitting on the edge of the bed, blood coming from the side of his head. He'd somehow fallen off the toilet and hit his head then made his way back to the bed. He was in bad shape because his kidneys were finally failing due to his stubborn need to drink. I called an ambulance, and he was rushed to Saint Joseph's Medical Center in Burbank.

He was holding on and coherent enough to talk to me, but it wasn't looking good, so I asked him what he wanted. "I want to live," was his answer. I nodded just as the drugs kicked in and knocked him out.

The emergency room doctor came over and told me he was shutting down, and it was only a matter of time. He asked me what I wanted to do while my father's last request was still ringing in my ears. Dad never signed a DNR or indicated what he wanted to be done in a situation like this. It was now my decision, and mine alone, to make. What he'd said he wanted and what the reality of that meant were two entirely different things. It was surprising he'd lasted this long at all despite his lifestyle and drinking habits. I needed to weigh his wish against the ramifications of him being in the hospital for months before he passed. I called his older brother Russ to let him know what was happening and that it wouldn't be long before he was gone.

A few years back, I'd considered the possibility that my mother's death was somewhat intentional and that she'd devised the perfect solution for all three of us. Her passing ended her physical and emotional pain; it released me from having to care for her and would allow me to move on with my life, and it placed the ultimate guilt trip on my father for abandoning her. Something he would have to live with for the rest of his life. She was a clever and highly intelligent woman who I believed saw an opportunity for abject closure once she'd been diagnosed with Type 2 Diabetes. It sounded crazy, but it made sense.

I finished my call with Russ and went back to the ER to tell the doctor not to do anything. Just let him go quietly and without pain. I knew my father well enough to know that he wouldn't want to live the remainder of his life in a hospital bed waiting for the end. Better he goes now without the suffering. He'd lived longer than anyone expected, and as a son who loved him despite his issues, he deserved some peace from his demons.

After his passing, I decided not to bury him next to my mother. I chose instead to have him cremated so I could one day scatter his ashes in the ocean. He'd always talked about his time in the Navy and thought he'd be more at peace amongst the waves. I loved my father, but I never liked him. That opinion might have changed had I spent quality time with him during my childhood, but I'll never know. Destiny, fate, or whatever you want to call it, intervened and kept us apart. I still grieve over losing him to the demon in the bottle and to a career he could never have hoped to compete with.

A NEW JOB & A WHIRLWIND OF THEATRE:

At the start of 2010, I was still looking for work, and we were still getting letters from the bank about the loans. Our next-door neighbors were of foreign heritage, and the wife was an accountant for an overseas employer here in the states. We were outside talking one day, and she mentioned that her company was looking for someone to spearhead a new operation here in Hollywood. She asked me if I was interested, and I said, "YES!" A few days later, I got a call from the company's director, who set up a lunch meeting at the Hamburger Hamlet on Sunset Blvd.

He explained that they wanted to have a more significant presence in Hollywood and needed someone who had contacts and knew their way around the studios. My resume' was impressive, but sales skills would also be required to secure new business. I assured him that my skill sets also included the ability to schmooze potential clients and then spent 5 minutes explaining what 'schmooze' meant because they had no such word in his country.

The man was eager to fill the spot, so he offered me the position with a salary that was less than half of what I had been making at MDS. Beggars can't be choosers, so I accepted the offer with the caveat that I'd receive a commission for any billable projects above a particular ceiling. He accepted the terms, and I was to start work immediately.

The company had already secured offices in Hollywood, so all I had to do was to report in and start establishing a foothold for an increase in film restoration and 3D conversions. 3D was all the rage, with almost every big-budget action/adventure and sci-fi film converting select prints to 3D. It wasn't cheap, and most of the work was being done overseas, where the 'per frame' conversion rates were less expensive. The overseas teams did excellent work, but most post-production mastering directors preferred not to travel abroad to supervise the conversion. High bandwidth digital upload/download setups were required to handle the large volume of encrypted data being sent to and from the company, and not everyone was set up for this yet. *ASPERA*, which launched in 2004, was the only high-volume system available, and the industry was slow to adopt it. As more and more films converted to 3D, the situation changed, and soon, *ASPERA* systems were popping up everywhere.

Most domestic 3D conversion work was done via SFX houses and post-production vendors. The work was tedious and often rushed to hit the outrageous deadlines imposed by the studios. And the end result was usually panned by critics and audiences alike. There were exceptions, but they were few far and in-between, with most people choosing the 2D version over its 3D counterpart at the box-office.

I chose to focus on the SFX community as they were the most involved and could benefit from the more extensive pipeline our business could provide. The aim was sound, but the company had competition from more well-known and aggressive studios also from overseas. These businesses were doing it the right way by aligning themselves with established Hollywood post-production companies or buying smaller ones to expand with their own staff. I tried to explain to the director that 'distance' was the most challenging hurdle we faced because there were too many local options available by his competitors. He was convinced otherwise, and it became a regular source of frustration for both of us.

The best part of my time there was working with Rick again. The company's office manager had left for greener pastures, and I brought Rick on board to fill the spot. No sooner did Rick arrive when the director decided we needed to relocate the office. I was lucky enough to find a space only a block away from where we were and made the deal. Rick and I were responsible for the logistics, and the transition went smoothly. Rick has been a stable presence in my life ever since we first met, and I'm eternally grateful for his friendship and support over all these years. Like me, Rick is also a film buff and soundtrack collector. It's not uncommon for us to have phone conversations that last for hours because of our shared knowledge and passion for music and movies.

***SHERLOCK'S LAST CASE: Photo courtesy of
photographer Lindsay Schnebly, 2009***

By 2010 I'd performed in eight Co-Op productions. 'A HATFUL OF RAIN" (Directed by Rebecca), "TAMING OF THE SHREW," "THE ELEPHANT MAN," and "THE CRUCIBLE" all cemented my return to the stage and my regained confidence as an actor. The next show, "SHERLOCK'S LAST CASE," would establish my ability to handle massive amounts of dialog portraying the role of Dr. Watson, who dominated the story.

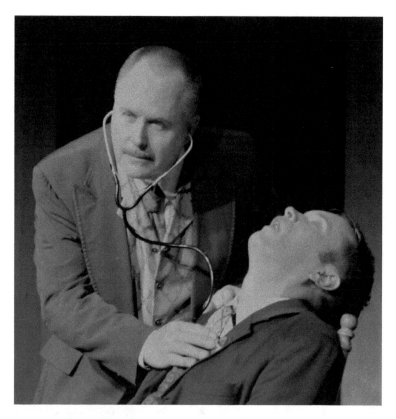

SHERLOCK'S LAST CASE: *Photo courtesy of photographer Lindsay Schnebly, 2009*

The talented Stephen Van Dorn played Holmes, and the elaborate multi-functional set was designed by Tim Farmer. Everything about the show was mysterious, moody, and inventive. I sunk my teeth into the role, using Anthony Hopkins as my inspiration for the needed subtleties and explosive insanity required for Watson's slowly unhinging resentments. "Sherlock" was followed by "THE PHILADELPHIA STORY" and then the role I was born to play in Neil Simon's "GOD'S FAVORITE."

The timing of this production was no mere coincidence. My father had just passed away, and all the anger, loss, resentment, and regret channeled itself through my performance. As a Neil Simon play, it was most definitely a comedy, but he'd written it after the death of his wife Joan, and it was intended to illustrate the pain of loss and letting go. The play is loosely based on 'The Story of Job'; *One night, a messenger from God, Sidney Lipton (with a big G on his sweatshirt) arrives, and, as in the biblical story, goes through all manner of temptations to get Joe Benjamin to renounce God. When he refuses, Joe is visited by all manner of afflictions imaginable. In the end, Joe ultimately stands firm, and the messenger has to admit defeat.*

GOD'S FAVORITE: Photo Courtesy of Photographer Greg Bell, 2010

Rebecca was cast as my wife giving us our 2nd opportunity to perform together as husband and wife ("THE CRUCIBLE" was our 1st). "GOD'S" Director had the set designed to resemble a 1970's TV sitcom setting complete with monitors and period commercial breaks to enhance the environment. The two leads, Joe and Sidney, share rapid-fire exchanges of dialog reminiscent of the old vaudeville days, with Joe plagued with comedic physical ailments throughout the 2nd act. It was the most challenging role I'd ever done. It was also the most gratifying. I didn't want it to end.

The reviews and audience response were phenomenal, and I was honored to receive an award from Stage Scene LA for 'Best Male Lead in a Comedy" that year. I've never been more gratified and fulfilled as an actor than when I performed in "GOD'S FAVORITE." It was a cathartic experience that changed me in ways I'm still discovering today.

My 9 to 5 work schedule at the company made it possible for me to do as much Theatre as I could handle, and the 2-mile office proximity to the Co-Op made it even easier. The Company Director was seldom in town, preferring instead to stay overseas. We spoke on occasion, but most of the time, I communicated with his wife, who handled the financials and accounts receivables. She was demanding and somewhat dismissive of my evaluations and recommendations related to the company's viability in Hollywood. I thought I'd been hired to provide knowledge and insight garnered from years of experience in the industry, but they seemed unwilling to listen to or consider any of my suggestions. By the end of 2012, it became clear to me that I was not providing them with what they wanted to hear, and a new General Manager was brought in to oversee the operation. I knew then that my days were numbered.

I think it took about 3 months before the Director had the GM release me. I was relieved that Rick's position was secure and left to once again find myself amongst the ranks of the unemployed. This time the stretch between jobs would last for three years. If I thought it was hard finding work when I was 52, it would prove to be a real challenge now at age 55.

It took the bank until 2013 to finally allow us to put the house up for short sale. For five years, we pleaded with them to negotiate an agreement that would enable us to refinance and reduce the mortgage to a more affordable payment. We continued living in the house without making any payments, but the bank was now ready to foreclose. The only concession they would make would be to allow a short sale of the property, keeping the foreclosure off our record and leaving us able to purchase another home in the future.

The lack of a mortgage payment over the past several years gave us the chance to put some money aside. Money that would now need to be used for moving expenses and up-front deposit costs for a new place to live.

We managed to find a small house for rent in Encino. It was quaint, well taken care of, and had a secured back yard to let our dogs run around. It also had a huge garage that would make moving from a 3500 square foot home into a 1650 square foot house possible.

"1940's RADIO HOUR" Photo Courtesy of
Photographer Lindsay Schnebly 2011

We both stayed active at the Co-Op through all this, with my taking roles in "THE 1940'S RADIO HOUR," "KING LEAR," "AND THEN THERE WERE NONE." There would also be two other outstanding productions, "A HATFUL OF RAIN" and "DAYS OF WINE AND ROSES," that I appeared in under the direction of my award-winning wife, Rebecca. Actor Jon Voight came to see "LEAR" because he knew the young man who'd played my son. After the show came down that night, he approached me, offering praise for my performance. It was an unexpected gesture and a compliment that meant a great deal coming from someone of his caliber in the business. I was really stunned when, just before he left, he came over a second time to shake my hand and offer his compliments again. If I'd been smart, I should have reached out to him when he was doing "RAY DONOVAN" a few years later. It might have been the start of a whole new career!

AND THEN THERE WERE NONE: As Wargrave.
Photo courtesy
of Lindsay Schnebly, 2012

REINVENTING THE WHEEL:

I'd registered with several domestic agencies that specialized in placing qualified people in positions with wealthy clients. Estate Managers, Butlers, Private Security, and chauffeurs were all jobs I'd done in the past for short periods to make money. Still, none of them ever stuck for the long haul. They were, however, all vocations that weren't hampered by age restrictions. In fact, age and experience were a huge plus. With my hair now white and with a beard to match, I cut the ideal image of what you would expect a classic butler or chauffeur to look like. When you added my acting skills to the picture, I created a character who was charming, distinguished, sophisticated, and, most of all, marketable. Many times, I'd been mistaken for Anthony Hopkins at Starbucks or an upscale restaurant when I was out and about town. The effect was flattering and only proved that it was something I could use to my advantage.

Side Note: *Over the years, the Co-Op had gone through several leadership changes amongst its Board and, more crucially, the role of Artistic Director. There was a small faction of members who saw the Co-Op as an opportunity to further their own careers. Play selections became more 'edgy,' and acceptable boundaries that our audiences could always count on were now being pushed to service individual desires and 'ego' projects. The Co-Op was never intended to be a platform for any one person's aspirations or obsessive desire to rule or influence its creative mission. Rebecca and I, along with a few other long-time members, began to challenge these decisions and were met with considerable resistance. The lack of an open dialog and willingness to see how things were straying from the company's original mandate made staying an untenable possibility.*

"AND THEN THERE WERE NONE" would be my final performance on a Co-Op stage as Rebecca, and I chose to walk away from what had been her Theatre home for 27 years! It was a painful separation that still resonates with her even today, some 8 years later.

NEW AMERICAN & THEATRE 40:

Our creative need for theatre drove us to find an alternate outlet, and our search led us to "The Odyssey" Theatre on Sepulveda Blvd. near Santa Monica. The Odyssey was home to 'The New American Theatre Ensemble,' who held auditions for new members/students under the direction of Jack Stehlin and Alfred Molina. It was a prestigious theatre, and Molina's involvement with the ensemble gave New American some gravitas in the theatre community.

We were a bit apprehensive about auditioning as we had been 'safe' under the Co-Op's roof for so long and thought maybe we were reaching beyond our capability with such a hardcore company. However, our fears proved to be unwarranted when we were both accepted as members and began attending class.

Jack was a talented actor with plenty of stage and television credits on his resume, and Alfred was every bit the consummate professional with a long list of memorable film roles. His list of awards is far too long to present here.

The class would meet on Saturday mornings each week with jack leading the proceedings. Alfred wasn't always available due to his shooting schedules and other commitments, but he did his best to come as frequently as possible. Each class consisted of physical and mental warm-ups, usually followed by individual and paired scene study. Not everyone in attendance would present during the allotted time, so watching and listening to Jack's critiques and suggestions of the presented work provided the bulk of the session.

New American was getting ready to produce Shakespeare's "A MIDSUMMER NIGHTS DREAM" at the Odyssey. Jack approached me about playing the role of 'Egeus.' I was never comfortable doing Shakespeare even though I'd done "MACBETH," "THE TAMING OF THE SHREW," and "KING LEAR" during my career. Luckily, Egeus was a pivotal role but not heavy on dialog, and Alfred was going to be our Dramaturg, so I readily accepted for the opportunity to work with him.

Rebecca was having difficulty getting past the fact that we didn't have the money to pay the membership dues required. She felt uncomfortable not pulling our weight even though Jack had waived them for us until we were back on our feet. I completed "Midsummer" and did two short pieces as part of their festival of one-acts before we felt we'd overstayed our welcome and left.

Towards the end of 2014, I'd also auditioned for membership at 'Theatre 40' In Beverly Hills. It was one of the oldest, finest, and most respected of all the small theaters in Los Angeles. With over 450 productions to their credit and over 300 drama critics' awards for excellence. Becky's best friend, Brenda's husband Gary, was a member there and encouraged me to try out. I went to the new member auditions and made the cut. Shortly after, the Theatre's Managing/Artistic Director David Hunt Stafford, asked if I would like to participate in the theatre's yearly production of "THE MANOR." TM was an Equity contract production, so that meant I got paid to perform. It was a unique show presented in the actual Mansion, where many of the real true story events took place.

Here is Theatre 40's Description:

A sparkling fictionalized re-enactment of actual events surrounding the Doheny family and the history of the Doheny Greystone Mansion. "The Manor" chronicles the triumphs and travails of the prominent MacAlister family during the 1920s as they ride the tide of good fortune. Spurred by legends of ghostly wanderings, costumed performers inhabit the Mansion's opulent rooms and roam its cavernous, echoing hallways to weave a tale that begins euphorically with the promise of a splendid future, but involvement in political scandal sparks a downward spiral that ends in a senseless tragedy.

The Doheny Estate (Greystone Mansion, as it's known) is located in Beverly Hills and is a registered historical landmark. The mansion and its surrounding gardens are open to the public and offer a dramatic look at privileged life during the 1920s, 30s, and 40s. Hundreds of film and television shows have been shot there, including *LET THERE BE BLOOD, THE WITCHES OF EASTWICK, SPIDERMAN, and THE BIG LEBOWSKI.* It is widely considered to be haunted, and tours of the house heavily emphasize the presence of nightly paranormal activity. Our dressing room was, in fact, the actual room that the body of Doheny's son was found after being shot. Creepy stuff, and I can attest to sensing something in the space whenever I was there alone.

TM was a delightful run, and one I will never forget. It would also be the last time I would perform for an audience. My life was about to undergo some radical changes, unlike anything I'd experienced up until then.

THE TRANSPORTER:

Becky's brother Jim often held parties at his home off Mulholland Drive. Attendees usually consisted of other Lawyers, legal friends, former clients of his, and whatever immediate family members could attend. His Yearly Superbowl party was always the highlight, and the one held in 2015 was no different. While gathering a plate of food from the kitchen, Jim introduced me to a friend who owned a Limousine Company. The possibility of my driving for him was broached, and I told him that I was interested.

I met with him later at his office and then began the training process required of new hires. Of course, as the newbie, I was given mostly Airport runs and late-night service requests. AMC was a client of theirs, so I would occasionally drive cast or crew members from "THE WALKING DEAD." I drove for Steven Yeun and Melissa McBride, who is an absolute doll. She'd never spent much time in LA, so I took her on an abbreviated tour of some Hollywood hot spots, including Greystone Manor. I got her to her lunch meeting in Studio City with Scott Gimple and then back to the airport for her flight back to Georgia. It was like spending 6 hours with 'Carol' without the zombies.

Another interesting client was Diana Galbaldon, the Author of the "OUTLANDER" book series. Diana had to be at Barnes & Nobel in The Grove for a book signing. Diana was a lovely woman, soft-spoken, and very engaging to talk to, and I thoroughly enjoyed getting to know her, especially since Rebecca was a huge fan of the TV series based on her books. Both Caitriona Balfe and Graham McTavish would also become passengers a few months later. Sally Fields and Jonathan Banks (BREAKING BAD/BETTER CALL SAUL) also graced the back seat during my time at TLC.

The Limo Company was OK, but it was never going to be a career employer. The pay was adequate for the time you worked, but the assignments were scattershot. I was the oldest driver in the stable, but all the younger chauffeurs had been their longer and were given better and more profitable trips. I was being underused and quickly grew tired of the inconsistent schedule and competitive positioning.

Before starting with TLC, my recruiter called with a one-week assignment to Butler for a small private group staying at a winery estate in Malibu. It was a Monday to Friday commitment with 12-14 hours of work each day expected. I would be one of two butlers, along with a private chef that was hired to prepare the daily meals.

The Estate was located on top of a small mountain off Kanan Rd. which winds its way from the 101 Freeway in the Valley to the Pacific Coast Highway in Malibu. The mansion had its own helicopter landing pad and looked like something right of a James Bond movie. In fact, the winery has appeared in numerous films and TV shows, including the 2-part series finale of 'THE LAST SHIP."

The estate had been rented for a week to a very successful Canadian businessman who amassed his wealth by storing and shipping produce to all nationwide Grocery outlets. He'd also invited four other friends to join him for the week. He was probably in his late thirties or early forties and was used to being the center of attention, so there was always something he either needed or wanted. The young man who'd made the arrangements for him was also a friend and had seen fit to include a Mercedes AMG G-Wagon as part of the package. It was a $180,000 SUV with a 577 HP V8 loaded with luxury that I wasted no time in commandeering for runs to the market and other places he sent me for items of instant gratification. Two of his friends arrived and departed via helicopter, providing me the opportunity to run under the rotating blades to unload/load luggage and offer assistance to the passenger. It's a silly little thing to mention, but it was a cool aspect of the job that I got a real kick out of.

Overall, the week proved enjoyable, with only one instance where inebriated behavior kept me there until after midnight because of a food fight. Whipped cream and custard-filled cake were strewn over the pool furniture, the tile floor, and the glass fenced enclosure around the seating area. It took me over an hour to clean up the mess after everybody staggered off to bed. I got home around two in the morning and returned to the winery seven hours later to serve the chef made breakfast at 7:00am.

On the last day after the guests had departed, the Grocery King handed me a wad of cash and asked me to split it with the other butler. The split came to $5,000.00 each for five days' work. Butlering didn't seem like such a bad career path after that.

CANOGA MOBILE ESTATES:

We were still living at the house in Encino by March of 2015, but our Landlord decided to raise our rent. I did my best to negotiate to keep it where it was, but he knew that someone else would be willing to pay more.

I'm sure by now you're scratching your head over the number of times I've mentioned moving in this story, and you'd be right to do so. For reference, I stopped counting after number 25, with Rebecca and I relocating at least six more times since we've been together. If you factor in the number of moves based on my age, it comes out to an average change in residence every 24 months! Change is inevitable, but that much change is just plain ridiculous.

In my search for home rentals on Craig's list, I came across a mobile home community in Canoga Park. They had several brand-new rental units much less expensive than what we were currently paying in Encino. It was an over 55 community with all the homes, except these two, owned rather than rented. The size and the price were right, so I hopped onto my motorcycle and took a ride over to see if they were as nice as looked.

A MAN AND HIS MOTORCYCLE, 2014

Side Note: *I'd been an avid motorcyclist since 1979 and owned a bike off and on throughout the years. I'd sold my last motorcycle back in the early '90s but wanted to get another after Rebecca and I got married in 97'. She, however, was adamantly against it, having had several friends in the past killed from riding. I put the idea on hold until 2009 when I was finally able to convince her that my soul was crying out to ride. I picked up a used Honda 1100 Sabre bagger before trading it a year later for a 2006 BMW Police RT-1150. The police bike had all the standard equipment except for the flashing red and blue and lights that were illegal in CA. I spent hours tinkering and modifying the bike with alternate 'legal' lighting and wore a white helmet with a boom mike attached for cell phone usage. The end result made me look exactly like a real off-duty police officer without the bike badging and uniform. When I pulled into the mobile park, everyone was sure something was going on that required a Police presence. Once the helmet came off, there was a sigh of relief from the small crowd of residents that came out to investigate.*

Riding in Los Angeles is a dangerous proposition at best due to unbearable traffic and inconsiderate drivers. Having the Police Motor actually made it easier for me because everyone on the road thought I was a real cop and would slow down, move aside, and even stop to let me through. It was like having an invisible force field around me. Of course, there were a few exceptions when some drivers would realize I was a civilian and not an actual cop. The resulting 'finger' or horn honk was a small price to pay for the added safety it provided.

The mobile home was outstanding, sporting two bedrooms, hardwood floors, and a master suite twice as large as the Encino house. It had a carport instead of a garage, but a storage facility just up the boulevard would provide the space needed for the garage items.

The park proved to be quite an experience with an eclectic cast of characters. As usual, we got involved in park activities with Becky becoming President of the Board's recreation club. She initiated a whole slew of themed events and parties along with 2 annual park-wide garage sales. The park had never been more active than during our time there, and everyone was sorry to see us go. Especially Dottie Correale, who became, and still is, a very dear friend.

THE BILLIONAIRE:

We moved in while I was still working for TLC and used the frequent downtime to organize and make the place a home. In June, my recruiter called again with an interview for me at a new Bio-Pharmaceutical company in West LA. They required an experienced chauffeur to drive the President and founder of the business on a full-time basis. They specifically wanted someone older with class and temperament, accustomed to working with extraordinarily wealthy and influential people. She knew I was just the guy for the job, and an interview with the gentleman's personal secretary was scheduled.

For reasons of propriety and non-disclosure due to the individual's wealth and stature, I will not be using his name here and will only refer to him as 'my boss.'

The first interview went well with a 2nd set a few days later to meet with the CEO. She was a woman of significant accomplishment in the Bio-pharmaceutical industry and was only a few years older than I was. We found some shared commonality in our life experiences, and I left feeling confident that I was precisely what they were looking for. Oddly enough, I never interviewed with the actual principal I was going to be working for. I'd briefly seen him pass by when meeting with his personal secretary but didn't formally meet him until my first day of employment.

The company had ordered a new Cadillac Escalade for me to drive. Obviously black, but with some custom seating requirements. The Caddy was delivered and dropped off at the office, parked in the PRESIDENT's reserved space for me to pick up on my first morning. I arrived with time to spare and set out from West LA to my new boss's home east of the 405. I knew precisely where I was going but hadn't counted on the traffic difficulties getting across the 405 Fwy due to all the exiting vehicles headed to Westwood and UCLA. The clock was ticking, and I was rapidly running out of time, facing the possibility of being late on my first day.

The pickup time had just passed, and I was now officially in deep shit. I finally broke through and punched it all the way up the hill to the house. There was an intercom at the front gate, and the estate manager answered and let me in. It was a short drive down an inclined drive flanked by tall trees that blocked the view of the home. When I reached the end, the house was now in full view with my boss standing by the front door, briefcase in hand. My heart went into my throat as I pulled in front and jumped out to greet him and open the car door. The first words he said to me were, "You wait for me, I don't wait for you." It was a chilling and precise response to my tardiness.

I immediately made my apology, but he interrupted by asking me, "Why were you late?" I explained that I'd left with more than enough time but getting from the office to his home posed a problem because of the excessive traffic I encountered at the 405. "Why did you pick up the car from the office?" he then asked. "It's what was arranged." was my response. That triggered a complete shift in his demeanor. "Oh no, no, no, that's ridiculous. You keep the car. It stays with you. That way, you can come directly from wherever you are rather than going to (redacted) to pick up the car first. I'll fix that when we get to the office. Sound good to you?" I was shocked. He wasn't blaming me and actually making it easier for me to pick him up going forward. I breathed a huge sigh of relief, and we engaged in polite conversation all the way back to the office.

His home was magnificent. It was of modern design crafted by a renowned LA architect. Its price was astronomical and was one of at least 4 homes I was aware of in the states and abroad. His wife was a lovely woman who had also come from wealth. The two of them together precisely fit the description of a genuine 'power couple.'

From that very first day, I assumed my role as both driver and protector. I'd quickly come to respect and admire him as I watched him work and interact with the staff. The company was growing at a rapid pace, nearly doubling in size in just a few months. Early on, I'd become a topic of conversation among many of the employees, who perceived me as a highly-skilled bodyguard and chauffeur tasked with providing round-the-clock protection and transportation. Was I former SAS or Swiss Guard? Even the FBI and CIA were tossed around as possible previous assignments. I was a mystery man who kept everybody guessing, and the attention just fueled my performance.

I was initially hired as an hourly employee with full benefits but switched to salaried with a bump in pay when my boss found out and felt I should be making more. He always looked out for me, and the trust we shared was something I held with great appreciation because I knew it was something he didn't give easily.

Early on, he and his wife had decided to beef up security at the house by adding round the clock guards on the property. There had been some incidents in the area that prompted many residents to rethink their security measures, and my boss was no exception. He wasted no time recruiting me to assist in the interview and hiring process of 3 guards for service at the house.

I got along splendidly with the house staff that consisted of a manager, a housekeeper, 2 chefs, and a houseboy that handled miscellaneous errands and property-related tasks. Upgrades to the security cameras and their placement around the estate also became something I got involved with, working with the manager and the surveillance vendor to bring their system into the digital age.

My days were full, and it wasn't unusual for me to put in anywhere from 10-14 hours at a stretch. He made a point of including me when attending business dinners (I would sit within sightline distance from his table), and I would often drive him and his wife to evening events, dinners at Nobu in Malibu, or one of the many upscale restaurants peppered along South

Beverly or Cannon drive in Beverly Hills. There was never a dull moment, and I was always grateful for his generosity and respect.

I'd started in July of 2015, and by August of 2017, the company had successfully completed clinical trials on a revolutionary cancer treatment and was purchased by another, much larger, Pharmaceutical Company. It was a monumental achievement that reverberated throughout the Industry and cemented my boss's reputation as a pioneering Oncologist in Immunotherapy.

ME AND AN ASTON MARTIN, 2018

There is so much more I wish I could tell about my time from July of 2015 to June of 2018, but I'm not at liberty to share any details or who the players were. I can tell you that late during my 1st year, Michael Milken came to our office to meet with my boss. Michael was a cancer survivor and one of the company's investors. It was a reunion that surprised my boss and seemed to elevate my stature even further because of my previous association with him. In September of 2017, my boss extended an offer for Becky and me to vacation at his home in Cabo San Lucas. All we had to do was purchase plane tickets, and everything else was taken care of by him. The house was situated in a private community right on the water and had the same elegant sensibility as his home in LA. We spent five days eating, swimming, snorkeling, and anything else we could think of while being waited on hand and foot. We had our own chef and a golf cart that looked like a miniature Cadillac Escalade to tool around the community in. We even had an on-call driver who picked us up and drove us into town for dinner and shopping whenever we wanted. It was a week in Heaven and a very gracious gift.

I wish I could have remained working for my boss. I felt that we'd formed a solid and trusting relationship that would continue after the sale, but he was moving on to new business opportunities that would take him out of state and out of the country for extended periods. My fulltime service would no longer be required, so we parted company.

Of all the nonentertainment industry jobs I've had over the years, this one was by far the most rewarding. Not just because of the money, but because of the respect and admiration I had for everyone involved. I'd never seen a more diverse gathering of cultures and brilliant people, all collaborating with such incredible focus towards a common goal. I looked forward to work every day because of the staff and their driven commitment towards research that would ultimately save lives. Their efforts made me feel that my part was vital because the safety of my boss was paramount to the company's success. His leadership was the driving force behind everything, and I was proud to have stood by his side through all of it.

At the end of 2017, we moved from our rented unit in Canoga Park to a purchased home at Oakridge Estates in Sylmar. I continued to have a presence at the company's new offices until June of 2018 and then took some time off to relax and reflect on the past three years.

Rebecca has now been at Disney for 25 years and plans to retire very soon. She's remained constant all these years while I've bounced from job to job, never knowing when the other shoe would drop and place us in jeopardy again. My rollercoaster ride of on-again/off-again employment would give any woman pause and reason to move on, but she's remained loving, supportive, and patient to a fault through it all. My love for her is absolute. No man could possibly ask for more.

ACT THREE: WHAT COMES NEXT

In 2008 Rebecca and I took our first trip to Asheville, NC, and fell in love. Kelley Hinman and Callan White are good friends of ours who were former members of the Actor's Co-Op. In 2006, Callan accepted a teaching position at Montreat College, and they relocated their family to the Asheville area. We wanted to visit and see what the town and its Theatre community was like. Once we got there, I was so taken by the Blue Ridge Mountains and the rolling hills of green that I went back 4 more times over the next two years.

It seemed that Asheville had somehow triggered my memories of New England, and I found myself drawn to the open spaces and slower pace of daily life. Gone were the anxieties I'd experienced as a child over the quietness and lack of 'city sounds' I so desperately needed back then. A desire for the quality of life over the quantity of it has become a goal that I'm dead set on achieving in the coming months. Between the scorching summers, the lack of rain, the fires, the earthquakes, and the traffic, I am done with California. After 47 years here, I'm ready for a change, and what I hope will be my very last move. God only knows I've done enough of that in my life.

In January of this year, before COVID was in full swing, I went back to NC again after being absent for 10 years. The trip was to see how things had changed and reconnect with Kelley and Callan and another family I'd become close to, 'The Liner's.' I'd also developed a relationship with a realtor named Debbie Applewhite, who I've stayed in constant touch with over the intervening years. My plan was to spend time with Debbie looking at properties of interest I'd seen on the internet. January was a deliberate choice so that I could see Asheville at its worst. All my other trips had been during spring and summer, and everything looked lush, green, and beautiful.

Seeing it in winter would provide me with a better idea of how the inclement weather and lack of foliage might impact my idyllic vision. Yes, it was cold and wet, but it didn't change my opinion one bit.

I spent one evening with Kelley and Callan while I was there, as Callan was busy splitting her attention between directing a production at Mars Hill College and rehearsing for a show at Asheville Stage. I can safely say that the Theatre community in Asheville is alive and flourishing, and I know it won't take us long to get involved and find opportunities to participate.

 The Liners were also busy, as their son Stefan is in the process of spearheading an investor package to produce a series of films written by him and his mother, Robin. They're a talented family that I'm proud to have as friends, and their continued support and prayers over the past 12 years have been a blessing. I'm really looking forward to the future prospect of spending more time with them once we settle in.

Jedi master Yoda once said, "Always IN MOTION is the future, difficult to see." I'd always thought he'd said, "Always EMOTION is the future," and perhaps all of the doubts, fears, and anxieties we're all experiencing right now make 'emotion' a more apt metaphor for visions of the future, all the more challenging to see.

<u>CURTAIN CALL:</u>

The journey I've taken while writing this book has provided me new insight as to how I'd always perceived my exit from show business as an end to my acting career. One simple fact is clear to me now. I never stopped acting. I simply traded the stage for the larger venue of life. Using my skills to both 'act' upon the opportunities I was offered and 'performed' my job with the same commitment given to the roles I'd played in my entertainment career.

Necessity truly is the mother of invention, and I've reinvented myself numerous times throughout my life to survive. I mentioned earlier in this manuscript that I felt I hadn't been given the necessary skills to cut it in the 'real world.' I was wrong. The abilities had always been there; I just didn't recognize them. My mother knew it, and at some point, I believe even my father did, but I would have to discover them on my own. I think I did a pretty good job and hope that they're proud of how things have turned out for me.

To quote Shakespeare......

All the world's a stage,
And all the men and women merely players;
They have their exits and their entrances,
And one man in his time plays many parts.

Here's to my next role and to someday, a long time from now.......one final standing ovation before the curtain falls for the very last time.

Printed in the USA
CPSIA information can be obtained
at www.ICGtesting.com
LVHW011349081023
760415LV00011B/132